Epilogue

Epilogue

ROGER H. GUICHARD JR.

RESOURCE *Publications* · Eugene, Oregon

EPILOGUE

Resource Publications
An Imprint of Wipf and Stock Publishers
199 W. 8th Ave., Suite 3
Eugene, OR 97401

www.wipfandstock.com

PAPERBACK ISBN: 979-8-3852-2110-3
HARDCOVER ISBN: 979-8-3852-2111-0
EBOOK ISBN: 979-8-3852-2112-7

VERSION NUMBER 01/06/25

Contents

Preface

EPILOGUE IS THE RESULT of a search for a home, a resting place for material written but not yet published. In fact, I thought the material was unlikely to be published in its present form with too little homogeneity and too much variety in length, subject matter, and length of time since individual pieces were written. Most dated from my time in Egypt—ten years off and on between 1980 and 2006—and in that respect, they were old news. I thought I had shot my bolt with *Niebuhr in Egypt*, *Masr*, *At the Margins*, *Middle East Tapestry*, and *My Story*. I had a fat and growing binder of pieces labeled "Pieces Not Yet Published," although my best critic suggested that they were the equal in quality and interest with those already published. And collectively they amounted to only about 110 pages. Logically, they belonged with *My Story*, another small book of 175 pages looking for some heft. But it was asking a lot of a publisher to perform the act of magic that would marry the two.

So, it was with some trepidation that I began casting about for a suitable publisher. I didn't have to look far. In an exchange of text messages, I explained my conundrum to the Wipf and Stock editor I had dealt with for years and he was his usual helpful self. "Don't worry about length," he said. Most books were too long, leaving the reader wanting less rather than more. "We'd be happy to do a second book! We can publish it alongside your *My Story*. That would be great! If you want to do that, go ahead and fill out the contracting document I've attached. . . . That'll get the contracting process under way." It was all and more than I could have asked for. Wipf and Stock has always made it clear that they made publishing decisions based more on merit than projected sales. This was no exception.

A second question was what to call it. I settled on *Epilogue* with its implication of a summing up or commentary on what has gone before. That certainly described that I intended to bring closure to the extended corpus that constituted not only this book, but also the previous five books I had published with Wipf and Stock. It is appropriate that with *Epilogue* I was revisiting Egypt, an old friend, and I hope that some of my earlier fondness is replicated. The celebrated light of Egypt shines as brightly as ever.

Finally, what about my approach? Couldn't the variety I have described above reflect a certain virtuosity rather than a lack of focus? Some are short pieces of four or five pages. Others take up entire chapters (see "Christmas in Ireland"), a little history or sociology, travelogues, of uneven length, occasioned by random episodes or incidents, humorous, often self-deprecating. It brings to mind a comment by T. E. Lawrence, who said of a colleague, "He was a caricaturist. . . . He saw the odd in everything, and missed the even."[1] The same formula that had gotten me this far, why change it now?

And there was a darker side. Egypt was not immune to the currents in the larger region. In late January 2011 unrest reached a breaking point. On the twenty-fifth of the month the January Revolution broke out in acts of civil disobedience by students and activists. There followed demonstrations, riots, and strikes, calling for the downfall of the Mubarak regime, whose reign was marked by increasing corruption and authoritarianism. The authorities in Egypt at first seemed to tolerate violence although they would later resort to strong-arm tactics. The old triumvirate—the Wafd, the Muslim Brothers, and the National Democratic Party (NDP), Mubarak's party—again contested seats in a legislative election. It had always been said that in a truly free and fair contest the NDP would finish a poor third to the other two. Previously, vote rigging had always returned an overwhelming NDP majority in the Peoples' Assembly. President Hosni Mubarak resigned on February 11 following eighteen days of mass protests that marked the beginning of a new era of political instability in Egypt. This was followed by another series of events that, in their trajectory, resembled that of other countries in the region: a vote that returned a slender Brotherhood majority, a brief period of rule by the Brothers marred by missteps that contributed to their downfall, a military coup, and finally a kind of coup within a coup, a succession of military rulers that ended with the regime of Abdel Fattah al-Sisi, who still rules today. Egypt is still desperately poor and deficit spending has dramatically increased long-term debt. The improvement in the infrastructure of Egyptology is a particular priority of al-Sisi and there is a new Egyptian

1. Lawrence, *Seven Pillars*, 57.

Museum, opened in 2023. For all the contribution to national pride, these improvements have come at a price: Egypt is still poor and still ruled by a pharaoh.

I

The Birds

I HAD JUST NOTICED my first bird in Cairo. It was not the first bird I saw but the first one I really noticed. He was a male *Pycnonotus barbatus*, or common bulbul, and he was sitting on the railing outside the dining room window. I noticed him because he noticed me. We stood and looked at each other fixedly for about fifteen seconds before he became bored and moved on. The bulbul is one of a class of small, dun-colored, passerine birds of Asia and Africa. *Passerine* means that they have grasping feet with the first toe directed backward. They are songbirds, and the source of stock references in Arabic and Persian poetry. But today there doesn't seem to be many of them, or other birds, in Cairo. With fifteen going on twenty million inhabitants maybe there isn't room for birds. The only other one I remember seeing in the city was a hoopoe, or *hudhud* in Arabic, outside a window at the office. Its crest was raised, a sign of excitement.

When I played golf at the Mena House in Giza on a regular basis I saw many birds. They were generally hoopoes, or carrion crows cleaning up an occasional dead dog on the eighteenth fairway. But it wasn't until Pakistan that I developed a real interest in birds. In the subcontinent they were spectacular, with pheasants, partridges, quail, pied hornbills, parakeets, and families of songbirds. It wasn't like some north American bird-watching event, where people stayed up for days at a time to catch a glimpse of a tiny, two-legged, egg-laying vertebrate with feathers and wings. These were *real* birds, and their names were as exotic as their plumage.

A pleasant morning could be spent in Islamabad wandering in the deciduous forest behind the Islamic University. There were not only birds, but Himalayan rhesus monkeys, wild boars, jackals, and an occasional barking deer. As the seasons changed, the broad leaves fell, the *jangl* became a sea of brown sticks, and the birds were easier to see. They knew it and I recalled meeting a male kalij pheasant almost naked on a footpath, before he hustled off into the underbrush. I bought a copy of *Collins Handguide to the Birds of the Indian Subcontinent*[1] and it was a constant companion on my walks.

It was the same in Niger. There I had a *Guide to the Birds of West Africa*[2] and it often accompanied me on my walks around the rice fields of Kollo. They bordered the Niger river and the birds were the only fauna that remained in this part of the Sahel. I was fortunate in having the book in Niger because there was almost nothing else to do. The birds in Niger were almost as spectacular as those in Pakistan. There were flashing pied kingfishers, little bee-eaters, and Abyssinian rollers like the Kashmir rollers we had seen on the Karakoram highway, with brilliant turquoise and blue below the beige outer feathers. There were also Senegal coucals, cattle egrets, grey herons, and sacred ibises. There wasn't a single ibis listed in the *Common Birds of Egypt*,[3] although they were among the most common themes in pharaonic reliefs.

I wasn't a serious bird watcher. But I was a student of the history of exploration and some of the most spectacular sights that Europeans met with in the early days were the exotic birds of South America and the Indian subcontinent. After the dull birds of Europe, they were as strangely different as cannibals in the jungles of Brazil or giraffes in Africa. But the book painted an unusually pedestrian picture. Of the 430 bird species occurring in Egypt, about 150 were resident breeding birds; the rest were either migratory or winter visitors. There were 123 color illustrations in the *Common Birds of Egypt*, but hardly an exotic bird among them. They were classified by their breeding habits. There were resident breeders, migrant breeders, introduced breeders, and former breeders. There were winter visitors, nonbreeding summer visitors, regular passage visitors, and accidental visitors. It read like a description of the European tourists that were flocking back to Egypt after the turmoil of 1993. Most of them were nonbreeders, to judge by the declining populations in Europe.

1. Woodcock, *Collins Indian Sub Continent*.
2. Serle, *Collins: West Africa*.
3. Bruun and el Din, *Common Birds of Egypt*.

There were a few old friends from Pakistan or Niger, like the great grey shrike, the pied kingfisher, the hoopoe, the common bulbul, and the rock dove. But they were a bland lot. Among the most interesting references in the book was to *Nicoll's Birds of Egypt*, the classic work on Egyptian birds by Richard Meinertzhagen. Meinertzhagen had been Allenby's chief of intelligence during the Palestine campaign in the First World War. He was responsible for the elaborate ruse that finally broke the deadlock on the Gaza-Beersheba front and allowed the British to crash through on their way to Jerusalem. It would probably be too much to give him all the credit. Like Montgomery later at El Alamein, the question was not whether the British would win, but only by how much.

But there is no question that the masked feint at Gaza opened the door to Beersheba. Meinertzhagen was mentioned by Lawrence in one of those incisive little character sketches that are dotted throughout the *Seven Pillars of Wisdom*. In return, Meinertzhagen savaged Lawrence in his own *Middle East Diary*, and the unflattering portrait was later used by Richard Aldington, whose *Lawrence of Arabia: A Biographical Enquiry* amounted to little more than character assassination. Meinertzhagen was an often-brutal man and his *Army Diary* was even more revealing of his character than the later book. He was posted to Kenya early in the war and spent the time pitting his Kenya Rifles against the German East African Rifles from Tanganyika. In a memorable scene, he surprised a German officer in his tent and shot him dead. After the war in Germany he met the man's brother who asked if, by chance, he had come across his brother in East Africa. Meinertzhagen knew the officer's name, having gone through his papers in the tent. He had to say no. The book is full of violent incidents like this one and violent opinions, a characteristic of the man. It was an odd combination: he was a violent bird watcher.

He was an Englishman of German extraction—the family had been bankers in Cologne—and not Jewish. But when he later became a rabid Zionist (he was always a rabid something) he was known as "that Jew." He became one of a group of prominent gentile Zionists that also included Orde Wingate and the Webbs. He had absolutely no use for the Arabs or for anyone who trucked with them. He spent a good part of the 1930s helping German Jews escape from Germany. He often traveled to Berlin and tells the story of carrying a loaded pistol to a meeting with Hitler and Ribbentrop. He says he seriously considered shooting them both. He didn't but it is interesting, needless to say, to think how history might have changed if he had.

Today the Nile was very high and muddy. It was the color of the Guadalquivir at Cordoba, like tea with milk. There had been floods in Upper Egypt earlier in the month, but below the high dam, so we witnessed what the Nile must have looked like in the good old days. Unusually heavy rains from 16 to 18 November in the Qena Governorate had led to flash floods and the water had come down in torrents from the mountains to the west. It carried away everything—roads, structures, and entire villages—in its path. Telegraph poles were found miles away from where they once stood. We had firsthand knowledge since the Arab Republic of Egypt National Telecommunications Organization (ARENTO) had sent one of the vice chairmen south to inspect damage to the infrastructure. He showed me pictures of the devastation.

Villagers had taken refuge in the mountains and many had barely escaped with their lives. Not the least of their problems was the plague of scorpions and snakes that were forced out of their holes by the water. Families lost everything. But there were probably still a few traditionalists who took some consolation in the color of the Nile. They had complained since the High Dam that the water was clear. It was not the Nile they knew and loved. Every year between July and October it had been *buni*, or brown, with its annual weight of suspended silt. On November 29, you could almost feel the texture of the water between your fingers. You couldn't see through it, though, and it was only the silt and salts from Middle Egypt, not the rich brown stuff from the highlands of Ethiopia. But still I wondered how the pied kingfisher would now see its prey.

2

Christmas in Ireland

AT LEAST THAT'S WHAT it was supposed to be. Laura and I would meet in Edinburgh and then we would just hop over to Ireland for a week or so. I had visions of a small bed-and-breakfast, brisk walks in the emerald countryside, lamb stews and pints of Guinness, tweed caps and woolen sweaters, curling up in the evening by a warm fire, and Christmas mass in that most Catholic of countries. It would be a time of reflection, of the slow perusal of a good book, and a chance for Laura and me to discover what we shared with Ireland, which was probably more Celtic than Catholic. But there was also the other part of the story. The republic was one of the success stories of Europe: per-capita GDP now equaled that of Great Britain, the migration of the educated—to anywhere but Ireland—had ended, and young Irish were coming back to find work. The software industry was booming, everyone was upbeat, the stranglehold of the church on Irish society was loosening, and Irish arts were flourishing. The Irish were expanding their chests and maybe my image of simple rustics in a timeless countryside was out of date. There may have been no place in the new Ireland for Paddy and Mike. But we wouldn't know because we never made it there.

Instead, the week was entirely urban, anything but bucolic, with relentless exposure on the television and in the newspapers to the domestic squabbles of Great Britain. It was as if the country was hanging out its dirty laundry for all the world to see. But it wasn't just the tabloids, and it wasn't scandal. It was the BBC. And *The Times*, now in color like *USA Today*, with its daily dosage of the banality of everyday life at this most stressful time of

5

the year. The front pages were full of stories of the victims of road rage, of children left at petrol stations in the Christmas rush, of old-age pensioners robbed, of presents stolen from under a destitute family's tree, a cut in the free-coal allowance for retired miners, of teenage bullies terrorizing their parents, complaints by Labor of the lewd baiting of women MPs by Tory backbenchers, and protests by the disabled over government cuts in welfare.

There were headlines like "A Victory for Gloom over Comfort and Joy," or "Fears Growing for Young Mother Whose Boyfriend Blew Himself up in Apparent Suicide," or "Father to Sue Hospital over Kidney Transplant Failure," or "Heart and Lung Boy, 10, Dies in Mother's Arms." It was ultimately numbing, as if a Siberian cold wave wasn't enough. But just to show that the British weren't entirely heartless, the government announced that after thirty years of residence in Britain, the payment of £3 million a year in taxes, ownership of Harrods, of the Duke of Windsor's former home, and sponsorship of the Royal Windsor Horse Show, Mohammed al-Fayed would be reconsidered for citizenship. But imagine the cheek! And in a television special aired to show the humane side of hunting, a fox was unearthed from its burrow and shot in the head *before* being thrown to the hounds, where it was torn to pieces. No, Ebenezer Scrooge was abroad in the land and Tiny Tim was nowhere to be seen. Actually, neither was in evidence. There was no *Christmas Carol* on the tube or stirring renditions of the *Messiah* or anything remotely religious or traditional. Instead, on Christmas Eve, it was *Naked Gun 33 1/3* with Leslie Nielsen and O. J. Simpson.

The week was all about those two late twentieth-century obsessions, communications and travel. If communications set the tone, travel was our constant preoccupation. If one made use of digital technology, asynchronous transfer mode switches, and gigabit speeds, the other seemed mired in the last century. The smallest unit of measurement seemed to be the *day*: from the time we left the hotel in the morning to the time we arrived at our destination, everything seemed to take a day. And at 56° north latitude at this time of the year, the days were short. On the twenty-fourth of December, the sun rose in Edinburgh at 8:44 a.m. and set at 3:42 p.m. That meant less than seven hours of daylight, on a clear day. But it was almost always overcast. We were always trying to *go* somewhere and, occasionally, we succeeded.

The country wasn't very big. It was only one hundred miles from Edinburgh to Straener and the ferry to Belfast, and that was the short way. But even that would take us all *day* and by the time we crossed the Irish Sea it would be late at night. And that was assuming that we could get there on, first, the train, and then the ferry. Nothing was guaranteed at this time of the year. *The Times* speculated that one-third of the population of Ireland was on the move over the Christmas holidays. I had to be back in London for the flight on the twenty-eighth, and *that* trip would take an entire day. But the trains didn't run on the twenty-fifth or twenty-sixth, so that left the twenty-seventh for London. It meant that Laura and I would have to return to Edinburgh on the twenty-fourth. But it was the twenty-first by the time I reached Edinburgh, and it would take at least a *day* to go anywhere. Let's see: Belfast on the night of the twenty-second, Dublin on the night of the twenty-third, and then the twenty-fourth for the reverse journey back to Belfast and then Edinburgh. That was assuming we could get reservations. So much for our week in the Irish countryside.

We originally thought we would rent a car and drive. But I had only my Egyptian driver's license and it was in Arabic. None of the agencies—Hertz, Avis, Thrifty, Europacar, Budget, or Mitchell's Self-Drive—would accept the Egyptian license without an attested translation. They suggested an international driver's permit. No one knew how to get one but suggested that I call DVLE, whatever that was. So, I called, and experienced the worst that American technology has to offer, except that the voice sounded like Margaret Thatcher's:

> Thank you for calling the Department of Vehicular Licensing . . .
> If you are calling from a touch-tone phone, please press one, now.
> Thank you for calling the Department of Vehicular Licensing . . .
> The following menu will be repeated in the event that you are not intelligent enough to understand it the first time.
> If you are calling from a touch-tone phone and are inquiring about licensing your vehicle, please press one, now.
> If you are inquiring about a driving license, please press two, now.
> Thank you for calling the Department of Vehicular Licensing . . .
> If you are calling from a touch-tone phone and wish to inquire about a new driving license, please press one, now.
> If you are inquiring about a medical condition which may affect your ability to operate a motor vehicle, please press two, now.

If you are inquiring about an endorsement on your present motor vehicle license, and you are under the age of seventy, please press three, now.

If you wish to make application for endorsement on a driving license on behalf on someone who is over the age of seventy, please press four, now.

If you wish to report a change of address, please press five, now.

If you require general information, please press six, now.

Thank you for calling the Department of Vehicular Licensing . . .

If you are calling from a touch tone phone and are inquiring about . . .

Oh, shut up!!

By the time I made contact with a human being, I found that I could have saved myself the trouble. Everyone knew that only the country issuing the original license could issue an international driving permit. What was I, some sort of idiot? So much for renting a car. But it was probably just as well. The north was blanketed with fog, the roads were icy, and the authorities recommended that motorists leave their vehicles at home. But I'm getting ahead of myself.

I had made reservations for the flight to London on EgyptAir a month before. The equipment was a brand-new Boeing 777, purchased to accommodate some of the hordes of tourists that were flocking back to Egypt after the troubles in the early nineties. In late 1997 there had already been over four million arrivals and tourism was the largest source of foreign exchange. But the Luxor massacre changed all that. The winter occupancy rates in the hotels in Upper Egypt—their high season—were now in the single digits. The front page of *Al-Ahram* periodically showed Hosni Mubarak chatting with *khawagas* in Hurghada or Luxor, as if nothing had changed. But no one believed that. Tourism was dead in Egypt.

I asked for an exit seat and was reminded again of the difference that legroom can make on a flight. The exit was next to the galley and the impression was of a comfortable seat in a medium-sized, very modern office. Everything seemed new, commodious, and efficient, and not even the indifference of an Egyptian flight crew could change that. I saw them in action in the galley and they spent most of their time dropping things, very nearly turning over a drinks trolley that had not been anchored. Little things like unsecured luggage on takeoff or landing never seemed to bother EgyptAir. In fact, three EgyptAir stewardesses deadheading to London were the greatest offenders, with flight bags littering the aisle under their feet. I remembered the Lufthansa stewardess who was almost physically sick when a passenger dared to leave a bag on the floor. But this crew were very pleasant, never allowing the presence of passengers to interfere with their enjoyment of the flight.

Over London, we circled in a holding pattern for half an hour and the next day *The Times* reported that the day before, the nineteenth of December, had been the busiest day of the year at Heathrow. Over 180,000 passengers had been processed. I had made a hotel reservation at the Westbury on Bond Street. The confirmation fax from Corin Burr, the reservations manager, offered a chauffeur driven "saloon car" to transport me from Heathrow to the hotel for £47, or about $85. A limousine would be £88, or $159. I took the underground. By the time I arrived in my room the trip had taken me an entire *day*, even with the two-hour time gain. The room was very small, about the size of the bathroom at the Balmoral, where I later stayed in Edinburgh. I freshened up and walked to the West End where I had dinner in a little Italian restaurant, mostly with theatergoers who had to make an eight thirty show. The proprietor-cum-headwaiter-cum-cashier called everyone *senore* and hummed arias as he worked. The English were exquisitely polite but the food wasn't very good. Back at the Westbury I turned in and understood why this room was offered for £99. It was over the underground and, even on the second floor, I heard the trains all night: *thathump, thathump, thathump, thathump, thathump, thathump, thathump, thathump, thump.* So, I decided that most trains consisted of nine cars. But I dropped off to sleep wondering why there was only a single *thump* on the last one.

The next day there was an errand at the British Museum, and, for the only time on the trip, I accomplished everything I wanted in a couple of hours. Many of the artifacts that Niebuhr had seen in Cairo in 1762 were now missing and I had unsuccessfully scoured Cairo for several of them. One was a black granite sarcophagus that was used as a watering trough. It lay in a recess under the steps of the *madrasa* of Qayt Bey near Qala' el-Kabsh, up the hill from Ibn Tulun. Niebuhr had spent a great deal of time making the drawing that appeared as a plate in his *Travels Through Arabia*.[1] The *madrasa* was still there but the sarcophagus was gone. There were similar pieces in the Egyptian Museum and they looked to be Ptolemaic or Persian. But the one with the hieroglyphs that Niebuhr showed wasn't there.

Then, in a bit of sleuthing that was as much an accident as anything, I found an interesting lead. I was rereading Lane and there, in *Manners and Customs of the Modern Egyptians*, was a description of a trough that was

1. Niebuhr, *Reisebeschreibung*, Tafel_030–35.

supposed to have had magical properties and had once been near the Qala'
el-Kabsh. Lane then said that it had been removed by the French during
their occupation and was now in the British Museum.[2] So, I had faxed the
head of the Egyptology department in London, with a description and a
copy of the plate, and asked if he recognized the sarcophagus among the
exhibits in the museum. To this there had been no reply. But I could always
look for it myself.

The page on the British Museum on the internet said that it was
closed during the Christmas period. But it was open on the twentieth of
December. They were remodeling the second floor and, at first, I wandered
through a warren of plywood passageways in the Egyptian section, before
a guard sent me down to the first floor. And there in room twenty-five I
found the sarcophagus, just as Niebuhr had drawn it, with a label that said
it was a gift of His Majesty King George III in 1802. And not only the sarcophagus, but also the broken, black schist obelisk that Niebuhr had shown
in another plate.[3] Niebuhr says it was in the threshold of a mosque in the
Citadel of Cairo. Nothing resembling it was in either of the mosques in the
Citadel in 1997. But here it was in London, also a gift of His Majesty King
George III, also in 1802. So, I looked through the exhibits for other similar
gifts and found four other pieces of the same provenance, also donated to
the museum by George III. They included the Rosetta Stone.

So, by one thirty I was done. But it was too late to leave for Edinburgh.
That would take nearly an entire *day* and the trains didn't leave in the late
afternoon. So, after a rest I joined the crowds on Oxford Street. There were
thousands of people but merchants were complaining that they weren't
buying anything. At London prices, it was no wonder. In a carpet shop on
Bond Street an Afghan copy of a Tekke Bokhara had been marked down
from £4,500 to £850. The new price was almost as outrageous as the old. In
Islamabad I had bought a real Tekke from Turkmenistan for $500. Dinner
was in the little Polish-Mexican restaurant I had seen in Mayfair the year
before. I still couldn't picture the combination, something like pork-knuck-
le fajitas. But it was all Polish: the kielbasa, boiled potatoes, and braised red
cabbage were good. I turned in early. My clock was still two hours ahead of
London and I wanted to get an early start for Edinburgh the next morning.

I was at Kings Cross/St. Pancras station in plenty of time for the 9:00
a.m. service to Edinburgh. Tickets for the trains in the United Kingdom

2. Lane, *Manners and Customs*, 394.
3. Niebuhr, *Reisebeschreibung*, Tafel_036.

were issued "subject to the National Conditions of Carriage . . . the National Conditions of Carriage are available at Ticket Offices." But in several days of riding the trains, and in spite of several attempts with ticketing agents, I never really understood the system. Scheduled departures and arrivals were not posted anywhere. Instead, they were available only in thick ledgers at the Information desks at the ticket offices. Questions required a great deal of cross-referencing, and prices and schedules were never available in the same ledger. One agent in Edinburgh flatly refused to give me the schedule for trains to Holyhead unless I produced a reservation for the ferry. I told him I didn't want a ticket, just the schedule. But he was adamant.

I developed a certain amount of sympathy for the ticketing agents, though. That morning in St. Pancras a Frenchman had a terrible row with a meek little agent involving a reservation problem. It was difficult to understand the problem because his English was poor and he was apoplectic with rage. But it seems that he had missed a flight to Paris and wanted to exchange the airline ticket for a train ticket on the spot. The incident occupied the attention of the entire, cavernous station for several minutes. I was standing, eating a croissant at a fast-food booth because there was, of course, no place to sit. So, the European Union wasn't so advanced that an airline ticket could be exchanged seamlessly, on the spot, for a train ticket.

I wondered what would happen to national characteristics under the new EU arrangements. It was like the latest joke making the rounds about the French farmer who found a pair making love in his field. He had hurried to the prefecture to report the incident. The prefect had reacted like a true Frenchman: this was spring, they were, after all, French, and these things happened. But that wasn't the problem said the farmer. The woman appeared to be dead. Now, this was serious and the prefect hurried off to investigate. But when he came back he said everything was fine. The woman wasn't dead at all. She was English. There would probably soon be a department in Brussels for the suppression of humor "which shall be construed as giving offense to any person . . ."

The trains were expensive. This wasn't like Spain where a first-class ticket for a six-hour, high-speed trip from Madrid to Granada had been the equivalent of about $29. It was like riding first-class on an airplane, with wide seats, stewardesses, and a movie. Here, a one-way, second-class ticket to Edinburgh, about the same distance, was £72, or about $130. The second-class ticket could be upgraded to first-class for only £9, if travel were on a Saturday, Sunday, or bank holiday. But that depended on availability and the seats on most trains had ticket stubs placed on the headrest, indicating that they were reserved. It was like reserving seats on the subway. And the service was about the same as they offered on the subway. They owed this to Lady Thatcher, who had privatized British Rail. There were now several private companies involved in providing the service, some responsible for the rolling stock and others for the maintenance of the facilities. That appeared to be a problem.

After I had entered a car and wedged myself into one of the few seats without a ticket stub, I understood that this was not British Rail at all, but the Great Northeastern Railway (GNER):

> Thank you for choosing the Great Northeastern Railway providing service from London/St. Pancras to Edinburgh/Waverly, with stops at Stevenage, Peterborough, Grantham, Newark, Retford, York, Darlington, Durham, Newcastle, and Berwick. Anyone without a ticket should leave the train at this time.

That was fair enough. But after the train left the station came the announcement that all standard GNER second-class ticket holders should be in coaches from A to F, except that if they upgraded to first class they should be in G or H since it was a Sunday. If they had a reservation. All first-class ticket holders should be in G or H, but only if they had a reservation. All super-value and weekend ticket holders must be in A to F since only standard GNER ticket-holders could upgrade on a Sunday. Reservations were recommended for seats in coaches A to F. Or something like that.

I had a Standard Saver Return ticket and didn't have a reservation, so I didn't know where I belonged. The same announcement was made after each of the stops and I was no closer to understanding it the last time I heard it than the first. Except that somewhere along the way there was a change of crew and I couldn't understand most of what the new voice said. The conductor punched my ticket without comment, so I stayed where I was, pinioned in a standard second-class GNER seat for the duration of the trip. But I never lost my fear of being evicted, hounded into another car by an irate conductor. Or, thrown off the train like some young Tom Edison.

The seats were arranged front-to-back on one side of the car, and front-to-front with a table in between, on the other side. But there was hardly room for a normal-sized human being in any of them. I was in the back-to-back side and there was so little legroom that my knees bumped the seat in front of me, to the infinite disgust of the pimply-faced girl who occupied it. Several times she turned and glared daggers at me. So I sat sideways. Luckily, there was no one in the seat next to me, and I occupied myself with the *Sunday Times*: "Comedian's Wife Gives Kidney to Daughter," "Family Despairs of Finding Bodies," "Bomber Magee Heads Terrorists on Ten-Day Leave," "Teenage Bully Says 'I Still Love My Parents.'" On the return trip I upgraded to first-class—it was a Saturday—and there was marginally more legroom. There was also a catering service, a gurney periodically pushed through the car by a pair of grim stewards. But everything they offered—biscuits, crisps, and soft drinks—seemed to be processed and wrapped in cellophane or foil. It wasn't very appetizing.

By midmorning the mist lifted and the countryside became pretty in a severe kind of way. The unplowed fields were a brilliant green and most of them were dotted with sheep. I didn't see many cattle. That was just as well for British farmers because beef on-the-bone was now "off" due to BSE. In the early afternoon as we approached Newcastle, football fans filled the coach, wearing black-and-white-striped jerseys with "Newcastle Brown Ale" emblems over the breast. But they were well behaved and there was no hooliganism. There had been talk in the papers of banning British football fans from the World Cup in France in 1998 because of their unruly behavior. Newcastle United were playing Manchester United that day. Manchester was in first place in the FA Carling Premiership and Newcastle was in ninth. I later read that Manchester won, 1–0.

Newcastle had once been the major coal center of England but the collieries were probably now closed. One of the reasons that the free coal allowance was being cut was that the government was shifting from British coal to the less expensive product from China and Korea. So, it seemed that they were bringing coal to Newcastle after all. There would probably be a court challenge since the miners had given up pay increases in return for the allowance. Coal mining, shipbuilding, and the manufacture of locomotives had been Newcastle's traditional strengths, none of them things in which Cool Britannia was competitive. The city looked grim and forbidding. When we came to a halt in the station the coach emptied, including the pimply-faced girl.

By one thirty in the afternoon, the sun was already low in the sky. Let's see, today was the twenty-first of December, the shortest day of the year in the Northern hemisphere. The sun would be at $23°26'$ south latitude. Assuming $55°$ north latitude at Newcastle upon Tyne, that meant the sun never rose very far above the horizon. And it was dropping fast. We passed into Scotland in the Cheviot Hills, although I missed the hills. The gloom deepened and then we seemed to go underground. At 2:45 p.m. the train arrived at Waverly station in Edinburgh. The Balmoral hotel was adjacent to the station just up the steps and a few yards to the right. They were selling rooms over the holidays for eighty-five pounds and Laura had made a reservation for me. It turned out to be the bargain of the week.

The room was huge, as wide as it was long, with fifteen-foot ceilings. The decor was tartan and the room key was attached to a heavy brass knob with a tassel. No flimsy card with a magnetic code or prepunched holes. The bathroom, as large as the entire room in the Westbury, was furnished with not the latest, but the earliest, in appointments: the toilet seat was solid wood, the basin was as large as a small tub, the substantial taps were of stainless steel, and the towel rack was heated. The shower head was five inches in diameter and released a torrent of hot water. The room was warm and inviting and I was almost sorry at the prospect of leaving it for a few truncated days of frigid travel in the Irish countryside. As it turned out, I needn't have worried. The Balmoral was home for the next five days, although they moved me two times when the room I was occupying had been reserved.

I called Laura and an hour later met her in the lobby. Her hair was still closely cropped and she was dressed in black. She looked like Sinéad O'Connor or Demi Moore. But it was more than an affectation and there was something substantial in her stern, uncompromising attitude toward the despoilers of the world and practical sympathy for the disadvantaged. I thought of Joan of Arc or, closer to home here, Oliver Cromwell. I later bought Antonia Fraser's *Cromwell: Our Chief of Men* and learned that the term *Roundheads*—those "who deliberately cropped their hair in scorn of the 'unloveliness of love-locks'"[4]—was due to a short-lived enthusiasm at the beginning of the Civil War and really did not apply to Cromwell's followers. Cromwell himself had shoulder-length hair. But I still thought of the term when I remembered the luxuriant growth that had once covered Laura's round poll.

She was her usual sweet self and, this time, there were no arguments. When she was with me in Cairo two summers before, we sometimes had discussions until the veins in our necks stood out. But this was the first time I was seeing her on her own turf and it was different. I don't think we exchanged an angry word during the week. And I had a real respect for her dedication. It was not a phase, something she needed to get out of her

4. Fraser, *Cromwell*, 86.

system. She took me to a little vegetarian cafe, very Berkeley with charcoal nudes on the walls and waiters with ponytails. Over heaping portions of soup and thick slabs of whole-grain bread, we laid our plans for the week. Then we went to the Information window in the train station where we had our introduction to the rules of travel in the United Kingdom during Christmas week. Ireland was out. Afterward we agreed that since the day was gone—it was now six o'clock and the sun had long since set over Ben Lomond—we would go back to the Balmoral and catch up on news. We had a great deal to discuss, including Laura's plans for her senior year. After walking Laura back to the student housing where she slept in her sleeping bag, I crawled into the oversized bed in the Balmoral and fell asleep.

We agreed to meet at Hadrian's restaurant in the hotel the next morning for breakfast. It will probably always be remembered as a symbol of wretched excess because the Scottish breakfast—eggs, sausage, bacon, mushrooms, and tomato—was priced at fifteen pounds, or twenty-seven dollars. They charged Laura the same price, even without the bacon and sausage. We must have passed the place twenty times in the next week and it was never without mutterings of outrage. After breakfast it was back to the room and the abortive attempt to rent a car. But we weren't defeated yet. We couldn't make it to Ireland, but they weren't the only Gaels around. There was always Scotland and we decided to go to An t-Eilean Sgitheanach, the Isle of Skye, just over one hundred miles to the northwest. The car ferry shut down in October and that left only the pedestrian ferry providing access to the island. The guidebook ominously made reference to the vagaries of the weather. No one could possibly want to go there at this time of the year. So, we made train reservations for the outward journey, paid a deposit for the Almonds Bank Guest House in Portree at the tourist information center and prepared to leave the next morning.

We were determined, even if it would take us an entire *day* to get there. The train would leave Edinburgh at 7:00 a.m. and arrive in Glasgow at 8:12 a.m. There we would transfer to another train, which arrived at Malig at 1:22 p.m., where we would catch the ferry. The ferry left Malig at 2:15 p.m. and arrived at Armadale at 2:45 p.m. Then, a bus left Armadale at 2:50 p.m. and arrived at Broadford at 3:30 p.m., just about sundown. From Broadford, a CityLink Skyways bus left at 4:30 p.m. and, winding its way through Luib, Scorser, Braes, and Camastianavaig, arrived at Portree at 5:10 p.m. The nice lady at the tourist information center told us to tell the bus driver to drop us at the top of Wakefield Road on the way into Portree. We could then walk to the guest house. All of this to go to a little island only 120 miles away as the crow flies. That was when we went to the information desk at the station and learned that the trains didn't run on the twenty-fifth or twenty-sixth. What was I, some sort of idiot? So, it would be Edinburgh for the duration.

When I woke the next morning, it was to a view of a sea of glass, the regular, undulating peaks that made up the roof of the Waverly rail station. To the left of the station, the Old Town, and to the right, the New Town rose out of the deep furrow that had once been a lake. On the heights to the left was Edinburgh Castle and to the right was the lesser elevation of Princes Street. It was an odd location for a train station, dominating, as it did, the view from the main hotel in town. But Edinburgh seemed an odd city and maybe it was only a question of perspective.

The city sat at the termination of the Firth of Forth as it came in from the North Sea. It seemed to be laid out anatomically. On either side at the opening of the firth—where the ankles might be—were File Ness and North Berwick. Then as the Firth narrowed—where the knees might have been—lay Kirkaldy and Musselburgh. Finally, there was the city of Edinburgh itself with its heights above and the dark cleft, or furrow, in the middle. Into this, the sun never penetrated. It was sometimes warm on the heights above, but it was freezing below. Laura and I once descended into the gloom, where hoarfrost lay on the lawns and the trees were stark in their nakedness. Our conversation became more animated and our steps quicker as if to make up for the cold. But we found only granite monuments to those who had given their lives in the World Wars. So, we hustled up to the relative warmth of Princes Street where our conversation resumed its normal cadence.

In fact, Edinburgh was a city of war memorials. We later visited the Scottish National War Memorial in Edinburgh Castle, which was billed by the guidebook as a stony vault of quiet contemplation or something of that ilk. There we saw bay after bay devoted to the memory of the Royal Marines, the Indian Army, the Royal Artillery, the Flying Services, the Household Cavalry, the London, Liverpool, and South African Scottish, the Canadian and Tyneside Scottish, the Cameron Highlanders, the Scottish Rifles, the Scots Guards, the Royal Scots, the Black Watch, the Seaforths, the Gordons, and the Scots Greys. The battles listed were an encapsulated history of the British Empire: South Africa, India, Flanders, China, Afghanistan, Singapore, Burma, the Sudan, Egypt, Palestine, Tanganyika, and West Africa.

Two in particular caught my eye: Kabul in 1878 and Kut Al-Amara in 1917, military disasters from which few returned alive.

Duty, duty, and more duty. But the notion seemed an anachronism, something out of the remote past like the heroic statuary that still stood in the old Soviet Union while everything fell apart around them. No one believed in it anymore. The feeling now seemed to be "give me a job and then we'll talk about duty." We met a few people in the city who seemed to be from the old school, striding purposefully and looking, it seemed, for duty—any duty—to fulfill. On Christmas morning on South Bridge, with its memorial to the men who had given their lives in defense of some corner of the Empire, a man actually wished me a cheery "Happy Christmas." Out of the blue. Just like that. I was so taken aback that I could only mumble something like "the same to you." But most people couldn't be bothered.

Not that there weren't laws to obey. Better yet, admonitions. Edinburgh was a city of admonitions: "Stay off the grass," "Danger of death. Keep out," "Private driveway. Do not park under any circumstances," "Do not enter," or "Closed." The last was the most frequent. Everything was closed for the holidays. The trains didn't run on the holidays, stores were closed for the holidays. Even the Holiday Inn was closed for the holidays. The produce shelves in the grocery store were empty—the distributors were presumably closed for the holidays. Nothing seemed possible and the answer to everything seemed to be no. I tried to have a pair of leather gloves repaired. The man in the cobbler shop and then the lady in the Stitch in Time reacted as if it were a grave imposition. What was I, some sort of idiot? We agreed that this wasn't a service society. We weren't the first to notice. A *Souvenir of the Opening of the Balmoral Hotel* in 1902 said it all when they included Dr. Samuel Johnson's succinct complaint in the eighteenth century of the stingy fare, slovenly service, and straitened accommodation.[5]

The Old Town of Edinburgh—pronounced "Edinburrrra"—ran the length of the Royal Mile, from Holyrood Palace in the east past Canongate, then High Street, Lawnmarket, Castlehill, and finally, Edinburgh Castle. It was architecturally homogeneous, all granite buildings turned black with soot, probably from years of coal fires. There were no exposed utilities and little vehicular traffic. It was established on a pedestrian scale and laid out for the out-of-town pedestrian. Along its length were boutiques and shops: The Auld Alliance, Cuttea Sark, Kilberry Bagpipes, Edinburgh Old Town Weaving Co., The Wyrd Shop, Wee Windaes, Scottish Gems, and the Scottish

5. Young, *Souvenir.*

Whiskey Heritage Center where tours were given in motorized whiskey barrels. It was all done tastefully and even the Holiday Inn's familiar green and white logo was demure and understated. We visited several shops along the Royal Mile where Laura looked at sweaters. Everyone's complaint was the same: no one was buying anything. Nor did we.

I generally met Laura at the corner of South Bridge and High Street, half way along the Royal Mile and midway between the Balmoral and the student housing. It was at the center of the city and we could elect any of the four points of the compass: north to Princes Street, east to Holyrood, south to Cowgate, or west to St. Giles Cathedral and the Castle. Most often we went south toward Blackfriars Street, Bedlam, Candlemakers Row, and Grassmarket. It was the university area and the places that were Laura's haunts: vegetarian cafes, grocery stores, and bookshops. There were also theaters and cinemas and on the second night we went to a movie, *LA Confidential*, based on a novel by James Ellroy and called in the blurb "the best American movie of 1997." It was a caricature of California, of bad cops and a prostitute with a heart of gold, with an unbelievably complex plot and gratuitously foul language.

It was a period piece, an excuse to display fedora hats and 1950s Fords, a kind of Southern California equivalent of the novels of Jane Austen. It was everything that *Witness* was not. *Witness* had the same stuff—corrupt police, romantic plot, good guy winning in the end—but it was a riveting movie. This was an embarrassment. What did the rest of the world think of us, anyway? The audience seemed to take vicarious pleasure in our extravagant use of foul language, our obsession with sex and violence, our preoccupation with right and wrong. In the end, for all of its surface sophistication, the movie was a simple-minded morality play, accent on simple-minded. The entertainment guide from which we chose the movie showed that another Americanism had crept as far as 56° north latitude:

> Key for film listings: (D) indicates that wheelchair access is available, although prior notification is advisable; (E) indicates the availability of an induction loop for the convenience of hearing aid users.

So, there were induction loops for the hearing impaired. What about the rest of us whose critical faculties were bludgeoned into submission by the sheer leadenness of the script? Maybe it was supposed to be a comedy, but it didn't seem smart enough to be laughing at itself.

The food in Edinburgh was good. On the first day it was Indian, the second day Scottish. They stroked their chins at the front desk at the Balmoral when asked if they served haggis in the hotel restaurant. They would have to check, and later said that they would need advance notice of two days! But haggis was available in pubs and stores and it was the taste treat of the trip. It was a compost of whole oats and the minced inner organs of small ruminants, lashed with suet and seasonings, laced with single malt whiskey, and sewn in a sheep's stomach. In the pub it came with *natties* or *tatties* or something like that, which translated into mashed potatoes and turnips. The tartness of the one mixed well with the blandness of the other. We later found haggis in a specialty store and cooked it in Laura's community kitchen. The microwave reduced the stomach to a shriveled, fibrous mass, out of which tumbled the steaming contents. But the taste survived.

The whiskey was good and smooth. I bought a tenth of Glenfiddich and it lasted me the week. It was expensive—twenty to forty pounds, or thirty-six to seventy-two dollars for a fifth. This wasn't like Russian vodka, and if the Scots drowned their sorrows in drink they paid a hefty price for it. I began to wonder if the expense wasn't really an exchange problem: the pound was overvalued, and maybe the prices weren't really as astronomical as they appeared to an American. If the pound were worth a dollar, prices, while high, might seem reasonable. Part of the problem was the rates in the kiosks. Like everywhere in Europe, the spread between buy and sell rates was huge: they bought a dollar at 1.779 but sold it at 1.616. It wasn't like Egypt, where the spread between the buy and sell was a few piasters. At an exchange kiosk at Waverly Station I bought pounds with a crisp, new American one-hundred-dollar bill. By the time a 9 percent "handling charge" had been added to the already punishing rate of exchange, I received £51.17, an effective rate of 1.954. It was highway robbery. The one-hundred-dollar bill was the repository of value internationally, held so widely that when the new bill was introduced the previous year instructions had to be printed in Russian and several other languages. Not here.

On the twenty-third we visited Holyrood—Holy Cross—Palace where the queen still maintained a winter residence. It was one of the sites proposed for the new Scottish Parliament. The guide, in tartan pants and a Balmoral cap, was a pro and catered to the national taste of each of us in the group—Americans, French, Singaporeans, and New Zealanders. Only the French weren't ex-colonials and they remained cynical throughout. We were shown sixteenth-century Belgian and seventh-century French tapestries, Persian carpets, and English furniture. The walls of one gallery were lined with a hundred gloomy portraits, a history of the kings of Scotland, all looking surprisingly similar. They were all executed within two years by a Dutch artist, James de Wet. With a look in our direction, the guide said that De Wet was to portraiture what Henry Ford was to automobiles. We replied that like Ford, De Wet apparently told his customers that they could have any color they wanted as long as it was black. Finally, there was the little room where infidelity, conspiracy, an Italian secretary, and a pregnant queen all combined together to produce dark *murthir*. The bloodstains on the floor were still visible after three centuries. It sounded Shakespearean, a welcome change after James Ellroy and a prelude to church on Christmas Day.

Outside, the ruined abbey was a moss-stained pile of granite. Almost everything was gone except for the shell of the walls and a single, vaulted side aisle. Small, irregular stones made up the pillars and the complex patterns in the ribbed vaults. It looked crazy, like the rest of it would fall at any time. Set in the rough cobblestones of the floor were stone slabs telling the identities of those buried beneath. These artifacts of medieval Christianity seemed almost as old as Stonehenge. It seemed a simpler time before the internecine broils that brought about civil war and regicide. There followed inflation and famine, unemployment, political instability, parliament discredited, corrupt politicians, the clergy preaching violence from the pulpit, and judicial murder. And the army, waiting in the wings, ready to step in and restore the peace. Pakistan or Indonesia or Nigeria in the 1990s? No, Britain in the 1650s. I wondered what Amnesty International or the IMF might have said.

We decided to have a Christmas dinner on Christmas Eve, since everything would be closed the next day. So, dressed for the elements, we made our way down to Bedlam and Cowgate where Laura knew of a French restaurant that might be open. She was in overalls, a sweater, a parka, a round hat pulled down over her ears, and sturdy climbing boots. I was in thermal underwear, Levi's, a heavy wool sweater, leather jacket, and leather gloves. But we never learned if the restaurant was serving or not. The manager was uncomprehending, from somewhere east of Suez but it was hard to say where. Maybe, I thought, Azeri or Armenian. He wasn't an Arab, and wasn't suave enough to be Lebanese. The conversation was a model of miscommunication:

"Are you open?"

"No."

"But you are serving Christmas Eve dinner."

"Yes."

"So, you are open."

"Yes."

"And you are serving a Christmas Eve dinner."

"No."

"Now, let me try to get this straight. Either you are or you are not serving Christmas Eve dinner."

"No."

At that point, we thanked him and wished him a Happy Christmas. But up the street was another branch of the same restaurant, although I couldn't imagine franchising this standard of service, and it *was* open. Here, the staff were all British. The two waitresses looked like the Spice Girls and were pleasantly inefficient in a ditsy kind of way. The kitchen staff were drunk and a steady stream of chefs and kitchen helpers made their way past our table with cans of beer and bottles of champagne. By the time we left, the sounds from the kitchen of laughter, of dropped implements and drop-kicked pans, had become familiar. But it was all good fun and the food was edible.

After the restaurant we did some last-minute shopping and laid in supplies for dinner the next day. At the supermarket Laura bought eggplant, onions, tomatoes, red peppers, and feta cheese for her holiday stew. Most of it was from Spain. But we had to go to the Bismillah grocery to find the lemons to give it the necessary tartness. I had the haggis. By the time we arrived back at her flat it had begun to rain and we struggled miserably through the dark, the cold, and the steady, slanting rain in our faces. We decided to cook that evening and it warmed us. Laura sautéed the vegetables and prepared a mess of couscous. I boiled the sheep's stomach for an hour. Then we watched *The Godfather*.

Christmas day dawned clear and crisp. We decided to go to church. Growing up I remembered a neighbor who said that he and his mother always went to church on Christmas. I was not impressed, full of the adolescent sense that one's relationship with God was a minute-by-minute affair, a new balance sheet being struck with every moral conundrum, of which life was full. What did they do on the other 364 days of the year? But here I was, now doing the same thing. Laura and I agreed to meet at the black granite heap of St. Giles Cathedral, up the Royal Mile from our usual rendezvous at the corner of High Street and South Bridge. I was in coat and tie and, as Laura approached, I saw that she had traded her bib overalls for a long black skirt and blouse.

The church was more welcoming inside than out. The altar had been moved to the center of the nave to bring the celebrant—if that wasn't too papist a term—into closer contact with the congregation. Otherwise, there seemed to be few concessions to modernity. There were no statues, and I was reminded of the Protestant detestation of idols. Cromwell was "so perfect a hater of Images, that he hath defaced God's in his own Countenance."[6] It was a reference to his bulbous red nose. But Cromwell would have had no more truck with these Presbyterians than with the hated Catholics. The prayer book furnished as we entered was that of the Church of Scotland, The Presbyterian Church of England, the Presbyterian Church in Ireland, and the Presbyterian Church of Wales. We entered the pew through a small gate, as into a stockade. There were no kneelers.

This morning service at ten o'clock began with organ offerings by Bach and Messiaen. The introit and processional hymn (no. 190 in our book)— "Christians, awake, salute the happy morn"[7]—accompanied the entrance of the choir, followed by the minister. The choir arranged themselves on the right, partly concealed by a cluster of pillars. After sentences and adoration came the familiar "Adeste Fideles" (no. 191). The congregation, sensibly dressed in a combination of Levi's, down jackets, and parkas, sang lustily:

> O come, all ye faithful, joyful and triumphant,
> O come ye, O come ye to Bethlehem![8]

Bethlehem. It was an odd thought here, a few degrees below the Arctic Circle. What were we doing celebrating the birth of a Hellenized, Aramaic-speaking Palestinian Jew? Yet we were, and all our Bibles and prayer books contained maps of the Holy Land, which most of us had never seen and whose ethnic complexity we would never understand. Religion was the reason, and there were even Scots who had thought of themselves as the heirs of the Israelites. Something about being one of the lost tribes. Language also had something to do with it. The rhythms of the national epic of a remote, stiff-necked people were captured in that masterpiece of English literature, the King James Bible. The first reading was from Heb 1:1–5:

6. Cleveland, *Character*, 6.
7. Byrom, "Christians, Awake."
8. Wade, "O Come, All Ye Faithful" [Adeste fideles].

God who at sundry times and in divers manners
spake in time past unto the fathers by the prophets.
Hath in these days spoken unto us by his Son. . . .
For unto which of the angels said he at any time
THOU ART MY SON, THIS DAY HAVE I
BEGOTTEN THEE.

So, we had our *Messiah* after all. The reader was a pretty woman in black coat and trousers, with dark, severely cropped hair. I thought, again, of Joan of Arc and of the sweet Roundhead sitting next to me.

This was followed by hymn no. 184, that celebration of sturdy burghers: "God rest ye merry, gentlemen, let nothing you dismay."[9] Were they "merry gentlemen" or were they simply to "rest ye merry, gentlemen"? And what about the gentle*women*? I could sense the insistent question beside me. The Gospel, Luke 2:6–20, with its "glad tidings" was then read by the same androgyne.

Then came the sermon by Gilleasbuig Macmillan, and it was plain-speaking and activist Christianity:

> Aye, there are the constrictors . . . those who would limit our compassion . . . I will have no truck with the constrictors . . . we must widen, not narrow our Christianity . . . not constrict our love for our fellow man . . . I have no sympathy for the creators of systems, the makers of creeds.

This was followed by the Apostles' Creed, that extraordinary compendium of Christian belief, which we were now invited to renew:

> I believe in one God the Father almighty, Maker of heaven and Earth, and of all things seen and unseen. . . . And I believe in one Lord Jesus Christ, the only-begotten Son of God. . . . And was made incarnate by the Holy Ghost of the Virgin Mary, And was made man. . . . And I believe in one Catholic and Apostolic Church: I acknowledge one Baptism for the remission of sins: And I look for the Resurrection of the dead: And the life of the world to come. Amen.[10]

I repeated the familiar words mechanically, not understanding them, neither believing nor disbelieving.

9. "God Rest Ye Merry, Gentlemen."
10. Church of Scotland, *Book of Common Order.*

Next was hymn no. 170, "It Came Upon the Midnight Clear,"[11] and then the offering, a small sack like a tea cozy passed through the congregation. After the intercessions came the communion. We were invited to come forward by stewards standing next to each pew in turn, opening the gate and permitting those confined within to approach the altar. Those who did assembled in a great circle, like some convocation of druids, while a communal chalice was passed from hand to hand and mouth to mouth. This, in northern Europe in the last half of the last decade of the twentieth century in a city where an outbreak of meningitis was a public health problem. I wondered about the position of the Church of Scotland on the doctrine of consubstantiation.

Communion concluded, events moved speedily to their conclusion. The remainder of the service included a Mozart *Gloria*, hymn no. 169— "Hark! The Herald Angels Sing"[12]—the benediction, and the *Noël, Grand Jeu et Duo* of Daquin. The principals—minister, stewards, and choir all dressed in medieval smocks—then filed around the pillars and out of the church. At the door we shook hands with Dr. Macmillan and wished each other a perfunctory Happy Christmas.

It had been the dose of tradition and high mindedness that we needed. To the believing it probably fell short of faith, but it was the best we could do. Then we went back to the warm, high-ceilinged comfort of the Balmoral to open the gifts we had wrapped the night before. By this time, I was in my third room in the hotel, having moved from one with a panoramic view of the old city and castle, to the roof of Waverly station, and finally to the traffic on South Bridge. The hotel had provided a red Christmas stocking full of fruit and nuts. We waited expectantly as each gift was unwrapped. I was already wearing one of a new pair of desert boots. Laura appreciated the coffee maker, the biography of Virginia Woolf, and the contribution to the sweater.

We agreed to have room-service breakfast. This time it was à la carte, scrambled eggs and smoked salmon for me and just the eggs for Laura. But why did they give you toast in those miserable little racks? The toast arrived cold and by the time we struggled with the frigid butter pats it was colder still. But the little jars of marmalade and blackberry preserves partly made up for the cold. The Scots were the greatest consumers of sugar in the world—greater than even the Sudanese—and we wondered whether

11. Sears, "It Came Upon the Midnight Clear."
12. Wesley, "Hark! The Herald Angels Sing."

there were any dentists in Scotland. After breakfast we rested, replete. The room was warm and inviting and we didn't want to leave. But there was still Christmas dinner and, in the afternoon, we went back to Laura's student housing complex on Kincaid's Court, heated what we had cooked the night before, and watched another movie.

The next day, the day after Christmas in Britain, was Boxing Day. It was supposed to be the day when all the boxes from Christmas were collected and put away for another year. All etymologies were suspect but this one seemed to make sense. It was also my last day in Edinburgh and we decided to make our only foray into the countryside. It was pretty tame stuff. Half a mile outside the city was Arthur's Seat, a dark pimple sitting a thousand feet above Holyrood Park and the palace. It was probably volcanic in origin. Laura had been to the top of other cinder cones in the area but not to this one, so we decided to make a midmorning ascent. We fortified ourselves with flapjacks—compressed bars of fruits, nuts, and oats—a reminder of the definition of oats in Dr. Johnson's dictionary as "that grain which in England is fed to horses but in Scotland supports the people."[13] We went first south, down to Cowgate and Bedlam and past the university. Then we turned east for a quarter of a mile to the base of the structure. From this perspective, it was really two peaks. On our left was a long sloping mesa with a flat stratum of alluvial deposits sitting halfway up at an angle of about 20°. And on the right, the steep cone itself, the top no longer visible.

We decided to head straight up the steepest part of the cone. The rain had stopped but there were puddles on every flat and soon the steps disappeared and the going became slippery. Finally, the trail became a miniature waterfall and we could go no farther. But to veterans of Kilimanjaro and the Karakorams, this was only a temporary setback. So, we retraced our steps and headed now east, along the north face of the cone. On the shaggy mesa below, tiny in the distance, we saw people and sheep. We watched as two boys on mountain bikes hurtled down a path before hitting the same wet patch in turn and spilling crazily.

The trail along the north face was wet but passable with, everywhere, patches of thistle, the national flower of Scotland. After five hundred yards we reached a saddle. To the left and below was Holyrood Park and above and to the right, awful in its majesty, was the summit. We turned to the right and now joined a steady stream of Scots laboring to the top as we were, but from the other side. There were men and women, children and

13. Johnson, "Oats," in *Dictionary*.

dogs. Occasionally there would be an entire family, mother, father, and off-spring, a bewildered infant in a backpack, its lips blue with the cold. But on we went. Out of the lee of the north face, the wind now picked up. It was all red faces, bits of cotton in ears and noses, tousled hair, and windburn. After a final agony, we reached the summit.

It was actually two summits, not one. There were two little promontories, one slightly above the other, with room for a few people on each. We paused on the lower of the two and surveyed the city and surrounding countryside spread out below. On our right was the Firth of Forth and beyond it, the North Sea. There was also Kircaldy and, in the center of the panorama, the city of Edinburgh: the old town below, then the castle, and beyond it the new town. To the left, there was a barely perceptible range of mountains and then Ben Lomond. There were two men perched on the higher of the two peaks but it was clear that they were not moving so we joined them. In the center was a little monument with a surveyor's alidade set in the stone. One of the two, ruddy faced and hardy, appeared to be using it as a prop for a lecture. He actually seemed to be enjoying himself.

But we were not. The full force of the wind had struck us as we reached the summit and it had not abated. And it was still bitterly cold. So, we joined the stream going down the way we had come up. When we reached the saddle, instead of retracing our steps along the north face, we plunged straight down toward the lake in Holyrood Park. The going now became treacherous. In place of the rocks the trail was covered with thatch, slick after the rain. I slipped once but caught myself. The second time I did not and after a graceful pirouette and splits, I sprawled ridiculously in a soup of mud, thatch, and sheep droppings.

At the little lake we watched the swans, geese, ducks, and pigeons being fed while I scraped off the mud. The pecking order was rigorously enforced. On the way back up the Royal Mile the shops were closed. But one pub was open and we refreshed ourselves, I with a tepid draught of amber liquid that was Scottish ale and Laura with a Coke. The bartender asked if we were here for Hogmanay, the New Year's celebration. There would be three hundred thousand visitors, he said, and people came from all over the world to drink, sing "Auld Lang Syne," and welcome the new year in Edinburgh. The press would be so great that tickets to the pubs were on sale now. As usual, I seemed to be going in the opposite direction from everyone else.

The next morning was the twenty-seventh, the day of my return to London. This time I had upgraded the seat to first class and made a seat reservation. The exchange at the ticket window was like something out of *Fawlty Towers*:

"I'd like a ticket on the nine o'clock train to London."

"Hmm, let me see."

"On second thought, what is available at ten or eleven o'clock?"

"Let's see. No, I'm afraid there is nothing available after the eight-thirty train."

"Not even on the nine o'clock?"

"Didn't I just say that there was nothing available after eight-thirty!?"

"Were you trained to deal with the public, or does the gift come to you naturally?"

"Huh?"

It was a wrench leaving Laura on the platform. We had thought briefly about her coming back to Cairo with me. But it was too soon after Luxor and there was still something that told us to avoid unnecessary travel to Egypt. And, in its own way, Cairo was just as cold as Edinburgh. The lows were about the same, even if the highs were not. And no one dressed for the cold in Cairo, although you did see men in overcoats and leather caps with ear muffs.

But we had had a good visit and had not exchanged an angry words during the week. In our prowling around the town we had discussed everything under the sun, from family news to sustainable development. I didn't want to leave her alone in that cold, dark little island. But she was a trooper, went the next week to Skye on her own and had a rare adventure bicycling around the island in the snow. As the train pulled out we exchanged a final wave and then the noble round-headed figure was gone.

The gloom lifted as we gathered speed and pointed south and I thought of another salvo by Dr. Johnson: "The noblest prospect a Scotsman will see is the high road that leads him to London."[14] In the first-class coach there were tables between all the seats and they were uncomfortable, although there was marginally more space for knees and elbows than in second class. Whoever did the ergonomic survey for the Great Northeastern Railway had his pencil sharpened very fine. There was tea and coffee and a refreshment gurney pushed through the cars: "Biscuits, digestives, rabita . . ."

The kid across the aisle was a talker but I was in a reflective mood. By the time he had ordered his third brandy and 7up he had moved on to easier prey.

14. Boswell, *Life of Samuel Johnson*, 129.

There must have been a following wind because we arrived in St. Pancras station just before two o'clock. My reservation at the Westbury was for the week before and, besides, it was a long walk from Green Park Station. So, I checked into the Green Park Hotel where I had stayed the year before. The room was tiny and the rate was punishing. There was probably a lesson here. The things we had planned—the flight, the Westbury, and the Balmoral—had worked. Everything else, and that was most of it, had not. And I was supposed to be training the Egyptians in planning techniques.

On Oxford Street the crowds were so thick that the Cairo habit of joining the cars in the street was the only way to make any headway. The tightly packed mass had a will of its own. London, Hobbes's "great belly, but no palate nor taste of right and wrong"[15] was alive with humanity. The stores were advertising bargains and sales were the rule of the day. But the prices were still astronomical and even the bargains weren't tempting. The papers were full of more domestic strife and mayhem. Another Johnsonism came to mind: "When a man is tired of London, he is tired of life."[16] But everywhere, on store fronts and in the newspapers, there were ads for somewhere else: "Easter sunshine, the mystery of Marrakesh, and the delights of the Canaries. From £699." Egypt had been the third most popular winter destination after Spain and the Canaries. Now, the big agencies weren't even taking bookings.

I had dinner in a little Turkish restaurant in Mayfair and realized over the cubes of lamb that I hadn't eaten red meat in the past week. I was tempted to find a slab of standing rib roast, beef on the bone, just on principle. The next morning Oxford Street was as empty as it had been packed the day before and I walked to Charing Cross Road before I found a place open for breakfast. It was a McDonald's and I had a sausage McMuffin. At Heathrow the EgyptAir desk was in a remote corner of the terminal and they had an exit seat. It was the same 777, the same crew, and they even recognized me. That was typically Egyptian, touching after a week of anonymity. Good old Egypt.

I had bought an *International Herald Tribune* in Heathrow and, after a week of *The Times*, it was a return to the wider world of the Asian collapse, ruble convertibility, the Unibomber trial, Le Pen's remarks on the Nazis, and the Great Game in Kazakhstan. Part of the difference may have been that *The Times* under Rupert Murdoch was trying to shed its elitist

15. Hobbes, *English Works*, para. 897.
16. Boswell, *Life of Samuel Johnson*, 378.

image. The new focus was more on lifestyle issues, appealing to a more youthful audience with features that were "relevant." In the fat Saturday, December twentieth, issue I had counted over two hundred pages, only the first twenty-eight of which really had to do with the news. The rest were, broadly, entertainment.

It was odd that casual exposure to one of the major cities of the world, vibrant and full of people of every complexion, with theaters, movies, and art galleries, only increased my sense of claustrophobia. With all the information out there in the ether, it took careful reading of an international newspaper, the oldest and most hidebound of the media, to restore the focus. Maybe McLuhan was right. We were now a global village. But the corollary was that we had all become provincials.

3

The Amadeus Chamber Orchestra

THE AMADEUS CHAMBER ORCHESTRA gave periodic concerts in the small hall adjacent to the main hall at the Cairo Opera House. It had been founded in 1991 "to provide its audience with spiritual, artistic, and musical pleasure through the works of the grand masters," according to the program, now lost. The founder was Samir Khoury, who was advertised as an amateur violinist and played a supporting role. The other players, about fifteen in number, were drawn from the Cairo Symphony Orchestra, and I noticed in particular the first and second violinists, the latter a Bulgarian young woman from Sofia. Most of the Europeans in the orchestra seemed to be from Eastern Europe, graduates of the Moscow Conservatory and similar institutions. Many of the featured Egyptian soloists had also studied in the old Eastern Bloc.

The concerts were generally on week nights and with admission at ten Egyptian pounds, or about three dollars, they were one of the great bargains in town. The concert on the evening of Tuesday, November 25, was typical: the *Adagio* by Albinoni, a pair of pieces by Boccherini, and the *Simple Symphony* by Benjamin Britten. It was all good stuff, very competently played. There was even a refreshing ingenuousness about the players: in the audience I recognized the Egyptian young woman who had given a Bach piano concert several weeks before and she was astonished that I noticed her. And this evening I had walked onto the Opera House grounds at the same time as the Bulgarian violinist and she seemed genuinely surprised that I was coming for the concert.

There was even a phenomenon like a "home crowd" with the concerts. They often showcased young Egyptian talent, and friends and relations turned out. They were vociferous in their appreciation. The greatest applause I had heard to date was for the young woman who played the Bach. But that was nothing like the triumphant performance of Mahmoud Saleh this particular evening. He played the Boccherini *Concerto for Cello in B Major* and he was eagerly awaited while the orchestra made its slow way through the Albinoni piece and then a Boccherini *Nocturne*. Then he appeared on stage, to an ovation from what appeared to be his own private cheering section in the middle of the hall.

The similarity to an athletic event became apparent as he strutted on stage, beaming and looking very cocky. He actually looked a little like Mohammed Ali, a very light café au lait coloring and his hair a mass of tight curls. This was going to be a virtuoso performance and you could almost feel the anticipation of his entourage as he settled himself with his instrument. He conspicuously carried no sheets of music. That was for lesser mortals and there would be no music stand to intrude between him and the audience. He gazed dreamily into the lights as Taha Nagui, his spare side locks flapping in the nonexistent breeze, led the orchestra through the opening bars.

Then Mahmoud attacked. He didn't just hold the instrument, he surrounded it, and there was something almost obscene about the embrace as he humped over to play the high notes. There was no poker face here. He emoted, gazing heavenward as he played the high notes, frowning at the intermediate notes, and positively scowling as he sawed away at the low notes. It was certainly an impressive performance. The program stated that he had "started his musical life with Prof. Ayman El-Hanbouli, when he was eight years old in 1987," and he had graduated from the Cairo Conservatory with a mark of excellent in 1995. Then he had played for two years with the Youth Mediterranean Orchestra and recently had been in Paris to take part in the International Cello Competition Rostropovitch. This was his first appearance with the Amadeus Chamber Orchestra.

But this was going to be a triumph regardless of his previous accomplishments. After the opening *allegro* he slumped in his chair, perspiring heavily and mopping his brow with a handkerchief. He dreamed his way through the *andante* before returning to the attack with the final *allegro*. The extemporaneous part seemed entirely improvised and it went on and on, while the members of the orchestra sat woodenly in their chairs and the conductor watched meekly for his cue. When it came, they resumed together and he finished with a final flourish to a thunderous ovation. The applause went on and on and soon little girls appeared with bouquets of roses. After the third curtain call, he seated himself again, surrounded his instrument, and played one of the Bach unaccompanied suites for cello. This was received as rapturously as the Boccherini and he exited, finally, in triumph. If he had been a fighter there would have been a woman, or maybe several women, waiting for him outside. But this was a chamber orchestra performance in Egypt. And he was only eighteen years old, so maybe the narcissism was understandable.

There was an odd appendage to the performance on this Tuesday night: a British group with the improbable name of I Fagliolini, winners of the 1989 Early Music Network's Young Artists Competition, and sponsored by the British council. They were *not*, as their droll spokesman pointed out, the Spice Girls. They performed pieces like the twelfth-century "O viridissima virga" of the nun Hildegard of Bingen, seventeenth-century plainsong and chants, "As Vesta Was from Latmos Hill Descending" of Thomas Weelkes, and contemporary folk music, all unaccompanied. The British contingent in the audience, a kind of counterpoint to the Mahmoud Saleh entourage, un-doubtedly enjoyed this particularly British genre. But as they made their way through the piece by Hildegard of Bingen, all I could think of was the Mus-lim disapproval of celibacy—"there is no monkery in Islam" as the prophet said—and the fact that Jerusalem had fallen to the Crusaders the year after her birth in 1098.

But if the previous performance was flamboyant, this was all British understatement and quirky humor. There were two Scots in the group so it really was British, not English. It was hard not to see in them the people who had thrown a girdle of strong dealing around the world, to use Lawrence's phrase.[1] The director introduced himself in execrable but unselfconscious Arabic and provided guidance with a running commentary throughout the program. It was easy to see why he was the leader. In spite of an awkward frame, long face with a receding chin and prominent nose, crowned by a shock of brown hair, he was the epitome of self-assurance. The gold signet ring on his left pinkie said it all. He needed no advertisement, his mere presence speaking volumes. He looked like a young Tory, that most favored of God's creatures, and he good-naturedly indulged the rest of us.

---

1. Lawrence, *Seven Pillars*, 660.

The other members of the group looked like they were probably La-bor. There were two basses, two tenors, a countertenor, and two sopranos. The two basses were big men as befitted the sounds that emanated from their large frames. Both had what appeared to be English names, although one had a heavy five-o'clock shadow like Richard Nixon's and dark curly hair. There must have been a continental, maybe a Spaniard, at some point in the family history. One of the tenors was very short and stout and looked like a butcher. The other had an almost unreal English look, light blond hair with no apparent beard. Shakespeare would have said that he had not yet begun to reap his chin. He looked like something out of *Alice's Adventures in Wonderland*, maybe Tweedledum or Tweedledee. His pants were too tight and his tuxedo jacket was too short. In fact, he looked like a particu-larly unpleasant schoolboy of the type that was once raised to assume, at the age of twenty-one, life and death authority over millions of subcontinental people.

The countertenor was also very fair, of moderate height, thin, with a receding hairline. The sounds he made were almost ethereal. The sopranos looked like two commonsense English young women, although one was a Scot by the name of Kennedy. She sang a beautiful Gaelic Christmas air from the West Coast. But the hit of the evening was Flanders and Swann's "Pillar to Post," a 1970s piece on the merits of the British postal box. The director told us that it was traditionally red, stood about as high as one of the tenors, and had a mouth, and he pulled apart his lips to make the shape where the letters were inserted. After this little introduction, he gath-ered the male members of the troupe around him and sounded the note with an instrument he first touched to his hair—it actually looked like a comb—before they launched into the piece. The lyrics were notions, most of which were inoffensive, and some of which were downright silly. It went on for several minutes and, after the last note, the audience exploded into applause. The director told us that the piece had a particularly English feel to it. He could have saved his breath.

So, it was an odd evening: Mohammed Ali on the cello, followed by choral selections from Monty Python's Flying Circus. I liked the first piece, the Albinoni, the best.

4

The Ballet

LAST NIGHT I WENT to the Bolshoi production of *Don Quixote*. Ballet tickets were expensive by Cairo standards, ranging from E£75 in the balcony to E£150 for the orchestra. Tonight, the hall was about one-third full. At an average of E£100 a seat, the take that night would have been about E£30,000 pounds, or $9,000. Assuming the same for each of the eleven performances of *Don Quixote* and *The Sleeping Beauty*, they would take in about E£100,000 for the two-week tour in Cairo. It seemed like peanuts. Expenses for the entourage—twenty-six soloists plus assorted dancers, twenty-two orchestra members, administrative staff, and coaches—must have been close to the take on a daily basis, assuming two to a room in a decent hotel. But maybe my estimate was low, since I went on a Sunday, not on a weekend. If they filled the hall and the average price was closer to E£150, the nightly take could have been in the neighborhood of $40,000.

I sat in the balcony where I could lean on the railing when I nodded off. The troupe seemed to be a showcase for young talent and soloists rotated through the performances. In the eleven days, there were ten different soloists dancing the two lead roles. The CVs of the principal dancers were included in the program (available at ten pounds), and individual photographs of the troupe, including the artistic director, the great Vladimir Vassiliev. There were also names like Aleksandrova, Ouvarova, Tigleva, Lavreniouk, Drozdova, Popovtchenko, and Bobrov, Most of them seemed to be born in Moscow, but other parts of the old Soviet Union were represented as well, places like Gorky, Almata, and Kiev. At the beginning of the performance, a woman in heavily-accented English had announced that they had just received word from Moscow that the "transcendent ballerina," Galina Ulanova, had passed away. It sounded like someone from the old Comintern.

The CVs included comments like "nice appearance," "possesses brilliant character-grotesque talent," "brilliant natural potentialities," "bright gift," "noble appearance, good school, and high technique," and "one of the young gifted ballet dancers of the Bolshoi Theater Ballet Company." All bore the trademark awkwardness of translation. It was like the personal ads in the *International Herald Tribune* for things like "a distinguished count of famous aristocracy" or "a charming Mediterranean beauty with great class, captivating in her youthful charm and feminine warmth."

I was tired and was not up for a full performance. After the lights dimmed I nodded through act one, slept through act two, and left before the beginning of act three.

5

The Parish Church of St. Joseph

CHRISTIANITY ORIGINATED IN THE Middle East and in Cairo we were surrounded by Eastern manifestations of the saving message of Jesus Christ. There were many Coptic churches in the city, although not as many as the Copts would like. They were licensed and the number was tightly controlled by the state. That was unlike mosques, which were everywhere, including little *zawiyas*, or informal mosques, in nearly every neighborhood in Cairo. The Copts were tolerated, and in the eyes of some Muslims that was enough. But there was no question of real equality and a Christian man who wanted to marry a *Muslima* still had to convert to Islam to do so. The reverse was, of course, possible without conversion. The pervasive, albeit subtle, discrimination was so odious to many Copts that they had left in their tens of thousands for Canada, Australia, and the United States.

That didn't mean that they welcomed others taking up their cause, and agitation for religious freedom in Egypt by outsiders was seen by most Egyptians, Muslim and Christian alike, as an attempt to embarrass the country. It was the one time when the tired old adage, that all Egyptians were one, seemed to be true. But in recent years the Coptic hierarchy had become militant, being full of ex-engineers and lawyers, educated men who, nonetheless, kept their militancy this side of the law. Occasionally, it spilled over and His Holiness Shenouda III, Pope of Alexandria and Patriarch of the See of St. Mark, was placed under house arrest by Sadat in the early 1980s. But there was nothing unusual about that, and almost everyone who disagreed with Sadat was thrown into jail. It was one of the reasons why he had been far less popular in Egypt than in the United States.

Cairo had representatives of the other Christian dispensations as well: Armenian Orthodox, Greek Orthodox, Greek Catholic, and Eastern Catholic, the last two in communion with Rome. Western churches were represented by Roman Catholic, Protestant Evangelical, Church of Christ, Anglican/Episcopal, Episcopal, Congregationalist, Church of Jesus Christ of Latter-Day Saints, the Church of Christ, Scientist, German Evangelical, Protestant/Interdenominational, and Christian Fellowship. They were listed alphabetically in *Egypt Today*, in their own section following "Casinos" and just before "Discos," and as long as they avoided proselytization they were tolerated by the Egyptian state. But in this cockpit of Eastern Christianity—most of the early church fathers had been Alexandrians and Alexandria itself had been a hotbed of Arianism—it became increasingly clear that the Christianity with which we identified was not a Middle Eastern, but a European phenomenon.

European included the American manifestations, although there was something about the Catholic Church in America that set it apart. It was a missionary and a building church with a bit of an inferiority complex. I recalled the pedant who was one of many Irishmen sent on mission to California in the 1960s. This didn't refer to the Franciscans and the Mission Trail but to America, the country still being a missionary area for the Irish Church. Not only was my religion a European phenomenon, but it was also a Catholic phenomenon. It was a little like the exchange in the 1963 movie *Tom Jones* between Thwackum the Vicar and Square the Philosopher. They were discussing their attempts to civilize Jones:

> Thwackum: I have attempted to teach him religion.
>
> Square: My dear Mr. Thwackum, "religion" is as vague and uncertain a word as any in the English language.
>
> Thwackum: When I say religion I mean the Christian religion, and not only the Christian religion but the Protestant religion, and not only the Protestant religion but the Church of England.

I felt the same way, except that it was the Holy Roman Catholic and Apostolic Church that I meant, although I hadn't graced the door of a church, except for weddings and funerals, in forty years.

This Catholic-centrism was reinforced by the cable television service we received in Egypt. There were three Polish, three Italian, three Euro, two French, one German, a Spanish, a British, and an American station. That meant a steady diet of programming from nominally Catholic countries. Even if the French or the Italians were not practicing believers, they knew what it meant to be a Catholic. Protestants *joined* a church. Catholics were born into one and spent the rest of their lives trying to get out of it. When Marcello Mastroianni was asked in an early movie if he was a Catholic he had just shrugged and said "isn't everybody?"[1] It was a kind of instinctive understanding that all Catholics shared.

So, on Christmas Day when I turned on the television and saw the French choir singing almost ethereally beautiful a cappella hymns, I felt right at home. The master of ceremonies may have been the thoroughly secularized and, for all I know, anticlerical little man who was one of the most popular variety-show hosts in Paris. But I understood that French combination of religiousness and anticlericalism, the kind of thing that allowed professed Marxists to send their daughters to convent schools. The Italian stations carried silly game shows most of the time, but occasionally in the Christmas season there would be something like *The Nutcracker* on Raiuno. The American station, the NBC Superchannel, offered the same hymns and the same sentiments. But you had to put up with a silver-haired divine who hawked Jesus like he was the Abdominizer. And he brought with him the usual collection of celebrity Christians—Fran Tarkenton and his ilk—all of them as impeccably coiffed as the preacher and speaking like they had taken lessons in enunciation at the Toastmasters. They probably had. It was not what I was looking for.

What I *was* looking for was experience of a society that was still existentially intact. I think I held America, for all of its goodness, earnestness, and uprightness, responsible for having destroyed my existential equanimity. Kierkegaard, Heidegger, and Sartre may have started it, but it was the Americans who seemed to take existentialism seriously, probably because of their goodness, earnestness, and uprightness. Personal responsibility was an awesome thing. I wanted to abandon responsibility and lose myself in something familiar, with all of its inconsistency. So, on this Christmas Day I wanted no earnest entreaties to love my fellow man, no Protestant appeals to do the right thing, no lectures from the chilly disputatious north. Give me a little good old-fashioned Roman Catholic obscurantism.

That meant finding a church in Cairo that would provide the right atmosphere. At first I thought of All Saints Cathedral on Abdel Khaliq Tharwat Street. But it turned out to be Anglican. So, I settled on the parish

1. Fellini, *8 1/2*.

church of St. Joseph on Bank Masr Street, just across from the bank. I did a preliminary reconnoitering and found that I had seen it before without really noticing it. The church had been founded by the Peres Franciscains de Terre Sante and was an odd combination of architectural styles, with horseshoe arches and *mashrabiya* in the windows and an octagonal dome. Most of the building was striped in the red-and-white *ablaq* style that had originally been Roman but was now thoroughly Islamic. In the façade, there were three Gothic entrance portals surmounted by paintings of saints. In a panel over the main entrance St. Joseph appeared with the rest of the Holy Family, probably during their sojourn in Egypt.

Inside, it was not particularly festive, probably because the interior was being renovated. Elaborate metal scaffolding was everywhere. It was cavernous under the 150-foot dome. The aisles on either side of the nave were lined with shrines, some covered with plastic to protect them from paint spatter. Candles burned in front of most. But there was a crèche to the left of the altar and a few poinsettias, concessions to the seasonal spirit. In the sacristy, a Franciscan told me that the services would be in Italian at ten thirty, French at noon, and in English at four o'clock. If Latin wasn't an option, French seemed to be the next best thing. The atmosphere in the church was decidedly French, including *Le Messager*, a *Hebdomadaire Chretien* that was offered for fifty piasters just inside the door. There was a *message de noel* on the front page and, inside, advertisements for various schools, orders, and establishments. Most of them were in Alexandria. There were the Salesians, Franciscans, Dominicans, and Jesuits. It was all familiar in spite of the language difference, and I recalled my astonishment at Berkeley when another student had asked me what a "Jessuite" was.

Le Messager included ads for a few old friends as well, including Lehnert & Landrock, a German bookseller on Sharif Street, and The Readers Corner, an Armenian bookstore with an interesting collection of old stuff, but none of it for sale. There was also a furnished flat for rent in Zamalek and an ad for Charcuterie Morcos, St. Mark being the patron saint of Egypt. Pork fed on fish meal in the United States didn't taste the same after the garbage-fattened pigs of Cairo. Many Copts had stopped eating pork, especially the mortadella, because so many had been infected with trichinosis. But well cooked, it was a welcome change from mutton and beef and Thomas in Zamalek had a good selection of filets, chops, and roasts. But the ham and bacon were too strong, with almost a metallic taste.

The atmosphere seemed perfect. If it was obscurantism I wanted, the combination of the language and that phlegmatic French approach to religion would suit me fine. So, I decided to come back for the noon Mass in French. That was another difference. Protestants went to services. Catholics went to Mass, and it was the same the world over. As it turned out, I wasn't nearly the cynic I thought I was.

I arrived by taxi five minutes late. I thought that probably wouldn't be a problem in Egypt, and it was not. People wandered in and out throughout Mass, some arriving forty-five minutes after the start. The priest was in the middle of a reading and it sounded like the Gospel of St. John:

Dans le commencement etait le Verb . . .

This was odd, since that was traditionally the last Gospel at the end of the Mass in English.

Par Lui et avec Lui et dans Lui . . .

But I wasn't sure since the acoustics were poor. The words from the microphone reverberated throughout the interior. There was all that metal scaffolding and not enough people whose soft clothing would absorb the sound. I made a rough count and there seemed to be about fifty in attendance. By the end of the Mass, an hour and fifteen minutes later, there would be about a hundred. It was a fraction of what the church would hold.

et sans Lui . . . il n'est rien . . .

Then, there were the readings by a lay woman. Her Egyptian-accented French was almost unintelligible. And the words were still bouncing off the columns and pilasters and architraves, beginning at the altar where they eventually returned after their jerky journey past the ears of the assembled. Not many of them entered my ears. There was also a choir, gathered to the left of the altar and out of sight behind a cluster of pillars. At first, I thought they were singing unaccompanied but afterward I heard an organ. Later I saw that it was a small portable device. The congregation were an interesting combination of Europeans and Egyptians. Many of the Egyptians seemed to be light hued and there were several women with blond or strawberry-blond hair hanging in long, beautiful ripples to the middle of their backs. It really *was* their glory in this, a country where a light complexion was still important and green eyes were the favored color in a mate. The family in front of me were more typical. They were a father, mother, and what appeared to be a maiden daughter. His hair was dyed jet-black but the white had begun to appear again at the temples. He was slender and of middle height and he wore dark glasses throughout the Mass. That was a Christian Cairo characteristic, dark glasses in the gloom. The mother was short and stout and dressed in black. The daughter appeared to be about thirty. All were sharply featured. It was very European this, the single daughter. They didn't have lots of children like the *fellaheen* in the villages.

They appeared to be existentially intact but I wondered what frustrations weren't harbored in the breast of the daughter. She probably still lived at home. I had always thought that Islam provided a coherent guide to life, although my attempts to express this to Muslims were always misunderstood, as if I was patronizing them. But I still thought it was so: God was in his heaven, he had given us a messenger and an example by which to lead our lives, and we looked forward to joining him at the end. It was very straightforward and had nothing to do with Islamism and people who were willing to cut throats over doctrine. These Cairo Catholics appeared to have the same sense of tranquility. And I realized that it was probably a cultural and not a religious phenomenon.

People were still arriving thirty minutes after the Mass had begun. They walked boldly to the front of the church or crossed in front of the altar to reach the crèche. There seemed to be no accepted way of doing things. People stood or sat or, occasionally, knelt as the mood struck them. This was very Egyptian, and different from an American service where a deacon—generally a fearsome female—controlled the movements of the congregation. Woe betide the man who didn't stand when she stood or kneel when she knelt!

I understood almost nothing of the sermon. The priest stabbed at the air in an unexpected display of emotion. At the Consecration, most people stood although some sat. Communion was in the old-fashioned way, little paper-thin wafers. The communicants gathered from every direction with about as much organization as the cars on Qasr en-Nil Street outside. There was a great deal of butting in. But, just like the traffic on Qasr en-Nil, everything eventually worked out and we all got what we wanted. I went to communion for the first time in years. That was another difference: Catholics *went to* communion. Protestants *took* communion. The wafer was so thin that it melted like a snowflake as soon as it touched my palate. Afterward, I decided to wander over and have a look at the crèche. Why not? Everyone else was doing it. When I returned the choir had broken into an English hymn, "The First Noël." The business of the Mass now over, the proceedings moved to their rapid conclusion. That was another thing about the church: the core of the Mass was the Eucharist and everything else was just window dressing.

> Noël, Noël, Noël, Noël,
> born is the King of Israel.[2]

The word *Israel* was an unwelcome intrusion into my European reverie. All I could think of were the economic woes of Bethlehem in this, the first Christmas season in thirty years that was not under the thumb of the Israelis. But then another one of those magnificent Christmas hymns, "Adeste Fideles,"[3] restored my serenity. I lingered, not wanting to give up the mood. I even lighted a candle in memory of a father and a son. By the time I made my way to the entrance of the church the French Franciscan was patting the last child on the head. Not even a thought of the church's awful problem with pedophilia crossed my mind. But what the hell was he doing out there? Protestants shook the hand of the vicar or the minister after the service, but Catholic priests were supposed to be remote.

And then it was back onto Qasr en-Nil Street. It had been particularly blustery the day before and everything that didn't move was covered with that fine Cairo dust. *Bawwabs* were bellowing, the standard Cairo form of address. The horn, that indispensable Cairo accoutrement, was given full play. Cars and people were everywhere, interchangeably, on the sidewalks and in the streets. I plunged into the melee.

The spell was broken.

---

2. "First Nowel the Angel Did Say" [The First Noël].
3. Wade, "O Come, All Ye Faithful" [Adeste fideles].

6

Amsterdam

It was my second attempt to fly to the United States through Amsterdam using KLM and Northwest. The first time, the Northwest strike intervened. This time, it would be KLM to Amsterdam and then Northwest to Philadelphia. On the return flight, there would be a twelve-hour layover, and with an extra day it would mean two days in Amsterdam, time enough to go down to Leiden and visit E. M. Brill. Leiden had been an early center of Oriental studies in Europe and Brill was a publisher of scholarly books on the Middle East. I was particularly interested in anything on the Jews of eighteenth-century Egypt.

The flight from Cairo was my first on KLM and the impression was not particularly favorable. At the check-in counter, I asked for an exit seat with extra legroom and the agent carefully searched the screen before giving me a seat assignment and a boarding card for both flights. Neither was an exit seat, which makes international flights merely uncomfortable instead of very uncomfortable. In my seat, I later calculated that I was wedged into a space of thirteen and a half square feet, or exactly half a square meter. My elbows were pinioned to my sides and I awakened from a fitful sleep on the approach to Amsterdam with the usual kink in my neck. The flight crew—all tall, thin, blonde, and female with the exception of a little black man from Surinam—were surprisingly inept. They boarded a woman in a wheelchair in the middle of normal process and we all stood, an increasingly long line snaking through the articulated walkway, while they wrestled her out of the chair and into her seat.

43

The meal service was a model of inefficiency, the man from Surinam carrying individual trays half the length of the cabin before returning to the gurney for another single tray. As a result, some passengers had finished the meal before others had even been served. When they collected the trays, they parked the gurney in front of one of the rest rooms and confined an unfortunate woman within for several minutes until her banging attracted their attention. When the seat belt sign was turned on for the final approach to Amsterdam, the stewardesses hammered on the doors of the restrooms and even used a little key to open them, with people still inside. It was appalling. They seemed to have the same no-nonsense approach as in Lufthansa, but Lufthansa stewardesses knew their jobs.

At Schiphol airport, I had a four-hour layover and did a little reconnoitering for the return visit. There was a train station in the airport itself and Leiden was only twenty minutes to the south. The trains ran several times per hour. I had lunch at the most authentic-looking of the airport restaurants and ordered what I thought was the most authentic dish on the menu, Dutch meatballs. They arrived all by themselves ten minutes later, hot and hard on the outside but liquescent within. There was no mustard, no bread, no butter, no condiments. I asked for bread and shortly afterward a plate with two slices of what looked like Wonder Bread arrived. The bread was extra, the waiter told me. Two very pretty blonde young women were doing a survey of customer satisfaction after the meal and in the comments section of the form I suggested that they get some decent bread.

On the return trip, we arrived at eight thirty in the morning and I wouldn't leave until about that time the next evening. There was a special on the executive floors of the airport Sheraton and the desk clerk insisted that I would be happy with the welcome drink and the free continental breakfast in the executive lounge without even verifying that I was an executive. But it was nearby—I didn't even have to leave the airport complex—and I checked in for the day. After a few hours of sleep, I set out in the early afternoon for a look around Amsterdam. The city was about twenty minutes away by train, a second-class ticket costing just over ten gilders, or about five dollars.

From the train station, the main thoroughfare looked like the West End in London or Fisherman's Wharf in San Francisco, with trashy stores selling souvenirs and postcards. But off the main drag it was picturesque enough, with little canals carrying water traffic crisscrossing the center of the city. The boats weren't like the gondolas of Venice, just very practical workaday conveyances. There didn't appear to be an overweight Dutchman, or Dutch woman, in existence. Amsterdam was a city of bicycles, with bike lanes in every street and bikes lashed to the little bridges that crossed the canals. Dutch women wore short dresses and, with mixed success, tried to keep the dresses from climbing immodestly up their thighs as they cycled. There were also a few Arab women in hijabs. Enveloped in long coats with high collars which made them look lumpy and sullen, they appeared as misfits in this very fit city.

I crisscrossed the little roads and canals looking for something of interest, bookstores or museums. Then I lost my way, wandering from the cute little canals and postcard facades into what looked like a light industrial area. I asked in a butcher shop for directions to the train station and the butcher, who looked like an Arab although the shop didn't advertise halal meat, pointed me in the right direction. By this time, it was nearly five o'clock. I was hungry and decided to look for a restaurant. After a beer, I asked the waitress in an outdoor cafe near the train station if she knew of a good Indonesian restaurant. She was from Chicago and gave me a name and even drew me a little map. It was near the red-light district, she said. I found the restaurant but it was closed. Anyway, the usual chicken in peanut sauce on the menu posted on the window didn't seem inspiring.

But there was a Portuguese restaurant next door and it looked interesting. It seemed to be run by a family, the patriarch tending bar and the mother and daughter waiting on the tables. They had the usual linguistic virtuosity of the Dutch, speaking to one another in Portuguese, to me in English, to other patrons in Dutch or French. I briefly thought of the history that linked the two countries, of the Portuguese Jews who were major financiers of the crown in the fifteenth century before being expelled, and how the Netherlands—not the Spanish Netherlands, which later became Belgium—had been a refuge for Jews from the Inquisition in both Portugal and Spain. I wondered what a Portuguese restaurant was doing in the heart of Amsterdam, and the story that had brought them there. But the waitress looked at me as if was crazy when I asked; why shouldn't they be here? This was 1999 and the European Union, not 1492.

I remembered Lisbon with starters of sourdough bread, olives, and anchovy paste, but here the bread was soft and bland. I ordered a dish of pork and clams and it came hot and sizzling, a mound of intermingled pieces of fried pork and clam shells with their burden of tiny muscles. After it had cooled, it was edible. After dinner, I walked through the red-light district, a small area of sex shops, theaters, and parlors, open to the street, where the prostitutes sat and advertised their wares. It was only six o'clock, long before the lights would come on in these northern latitudes, and only two Africans seemed to be open for business.

The next morning, I left for Leiden at nine. The train ride was about the same distance as the ride to Amsterdam the day before. The land seemed intensely cultivated, including what looked like potatoes and wheat. There was an information kiosk outside the train station but the young woman had never heard of E. M. Brill, and the university was not located in any one place.

"It is all over the city," she said.

So, I began walking, and it was a pretty city with cobblestone streets, canals, and an occasional windmill looking like something out of *Don Quixote*, not the high-tech devices of the Altamont Pass. There were the same bicycles as in Amsterdam, but only a few foreigners. Many of the young women had tattoos on their shoulders or arms. But there was nothing that looked like a good bookshop or a university area. So, I stopped in a drugstore and the druggist was very helpful, looking up the name in the phone book—it was listed under Royal Brill—and then consulting a map of the city. He wrote the address on a slip of paper. I should continue in the direction I was going for about half an hour, he thought, through an area of residences and light industry. It was now about ten o'clock, but by ten thirty, I had passed a train station and into an area of auto dealerships. No one on the street had heard of Brill. So, I retraced my steps to the city center and asked another druggist. Yes, she said, after looking at the address, I had been going in the right direction but needed to go farther.

I returned past the dealerships, the massive brick steeple of a church, and little row houses with Indonesian artifacts in the window. But now I went on into the country, past a canal with a drawbridge raised to let a barge pass, and into another area of industrial parks. It was now noon and I could feel a serious blister forming on my right heel. There wasn't a taxi in sight and it was no use going further on foot, and I even wondered if I could make it back to the center of the city. Very gingerly, I made the return trip and then walked around the area of little canals looking for bookstores. I found a single one, selling new books, and bought *The Death of Yugoslavia* and *Kosovo: A Short History*.[1] So much for the Jews of eighteenth-century Egypt.

1. Silber and Little, *Death of Yugoslavia*; and Malcolm, *Kosovo*.

I arrived back at the airport in time to eat, collect my bags, and check in for the evening flight to Cairo. I was hungry, not having eaten all day, and decided to try again for an authentic meal. The restaurant in the Sheraton was almost empty, and I should have been warned. But it had an interesting menu and I ordered venison with mushrooms, with visions of the scene from *Robin Hood* with Errol Flynn tucking into a great joint of game, with a side dish of huge, floppy mushrooms.[2] I had just left America where portions in restaurants were gargantuan, with a clientele that sometimes matched the meal. But when the venison arrived it was minuscule, maybe four ounces of unidentifiable, purple meat in a little cube. Actually, the presentation was very American, but Californian, not Midwestern cuisine. The cube was sitting in the middle of a little puddle of mashed potatoes, that itself sat in a slightly larger puddle of gravy. On top and in the middle of the cube was what looked like a piece of very thin, fried bread, formed into a kind of curlicue.

That was it. No bread and butter, no vegetable. I asked the waiter for bread and he brought just that, two hard rolls, but no butter. I tried to ration the cube but it disappeared quickly. Then the mushrooms, which I had forgotten about, arrived. They came in a small, oven-ready cup, two inches in diameter. On the top were bread crumbs and underneath I found the little mushrooms slices, just as they had come out of the can. I paid the fifty-nine gilders (or about thirty dollars) and left. Everything in this country seemed somehow off.

At the departure gate, sitting across from a hugely fat man, I was reintroduced to Egypt. He had taken off his shoes and his ankles were as big around as my thighs. The entire airport was a no-smoking area but he, of course, was smoking. Then a bearded man who looked like an Azhar Sheikh, wearing a long gray gown and a red cap like a cardinal's miter, wound tightly with a white turban, sat down next to me. Another Egyptian approached and struck up a conversation with the sheikh.

"As salaam aleikum."

"W'al-aleikum as-salaam wa rahmat ullahi wa barrakatu."

After a day and a half of incomprehensible Dutch, the words were as clear to me as my own language. The man worked in the airport in Amsterdam as a baggage handler, but the Sheikh called him *ya bash mohandis*, or "esteemed engineer." Their conversation was a polite inquiry as to what each was doing and then they moved to a discussion of the state of Islam in Europe. One of the fondest dreams of Muslims was that Europeans, finding

2. Curtiz and Keighley, *Adventures of Robin Hood*.

empty the secularism I had seen all around me in the Netherlands, were adopting the saving religion in great numbers. But it was the dream that was empty and, for that reason, I found it touching and a little pathetic.

7

Salesmen

THE EGYPTIANS HAD A reputation, probably undeserved, for being poor salesmen. This was probably because we dealt with a public sector entity that provided a service that only one in twenty Egyptians had: a telephone. They didn't need to sell the service. In a country of some sixty million there were about a million telephones connected to subscribers and a waiting list of over three million. And that was just expressed demand, a measure of people who had taken the trouble to register, with the wait measured in years. In Cairo in late 1997 the minister announced that Telecom Egypt was filling the waiting list of 1993, and this was after feverish building activity of the previous five years. There was also a *khidma faowriya*, or instant connection scheme, where a residential customer could pay two thousand pounds (about six hundred dollars) to be connected in forty-five days. For a business customer the same service cost four thousand pounds. We tried to interest Telecom Egypt in marketing, which we told them was not the same thing as sales. But we had little success. To indulge us they appointed a general manager of marketing, but he had no staff and no interest in the subject. He had laughed in one of the early meetings and said that the telephone company didn't need customers. "They need us," he said.

He had a point. But their revenue per line was a fraction of what it could have been, even without removing the subsidy to the domestic subscribers. They had advanced features on the new digital switches and they were now 75 percent digitized and a small but affluent middle class was able to afford them. And the forces arrayed against the old international accounting rates, on which they depended for 50 percent of their revenues, were increasing on a daily basis. Callback had already cut into their market. The ITU and the WTO were calling for a reduction in the rates. And the FCC had already announced that over a period of four years it would unilaterally reduce the amounts American companies would pay, in particular, for calls they terminated to developing world telecommunications monopolies.

Telecom Egypt charged a customer E£6 (or a $1.75) per minute for a call to the United States. The FCC estimated that the cost to terminate the call was about seventeen cents. The spread was huge and was going to come down, whether Telecom Egypt liked it or not. But getting them to recognize the fact was difficult. There were a few far-sighted executives in the company who actually tried to manage. But the rest were too busy to think about the future. The more senior they became, the more detail work they were required to do. That meant there was little time to think, and there was little delegation. We tried to interest them in planning, also without much success. Armies of ex-AT&T fundamental planners had passed through the company in the eighties without noticeable effect. So, it was no wonder that they had no sense of the market.

But any unsuspecting American—and we seemed to be especially vulnerable—who walked out the back entrance of the Nile Hilton knew that Egyptians could sell. The American may not have known it at the beginning but he understood, to his regret, after exposure to one of the pirates who lay in wait beyond the parking lot. Most Americans could handle the taxi drivers who parked near the big hotels, and realized that they charged a premium for their services. But they were defenseless against the street hustlers. These guys generally spoke good American English, with any regional accent you wanted. They all seemed to have a relative in New Jersey or wherever the American was from because that was their opening line:

"Hey, what state are you from?"

"New Jersey."

"Really? I have an uncle in Jersey City. Where exactly are you from?"

Answering was the first mistake. Americans are friendly by nature and can't resist this kind of thing. Others were not. Europeans were far more cynical and Asians were completely impervious to the ploy. But Americans were the perfect victims. By the time the salesman had finished with him, the American had drunk a cup of tea in his shop, chatted for half an hour, and left one hundred dollars poorer with a bottle of concentrated perfume he didn't know he wanted. It was only afterward—like waking up with a hangover and wondering where he had been the night before—that he realized he had been taken.

My favorites were the practitioners of the soft sell. Like the perfume peddlers, the hawkers in the Khan el-Khalili were transparent. But it was the small tradesmen whose pitch was just a wink or a nod that were most interesting. You could see by their eyes what they wanted. The shoeshine boys never looked at you directly, only at your shoes. They must see thousands of pairs of shoes every day, black ones, brown ones, slippers, sandals, buff, suede, and patent leather. They could tell at a glance which were the likely customers, as in "here comes a live one." The come-on was subtle, something like slapping the fold-down top of the shoeshine box against the side. A shine for a *khawaga* cost a pound. The same thing cost an Egyptian fifty piasters, but it didn't seem unfair.

I generally had my shoes shined in the morning while I read *Al-Ahram* near the Sheraton Circle; it was a good shine but not a great shine. It wasn't like Portugal, where they had leather inserts to protect your socks from stray polish. But it cost much more in Portugal. For some reason the shoeshine boy in Cairo came to the conclusion that I was Spanish, so every morning he asked me how things were in *Espanya*. We spoke Arabic so he never knew that I didn't understand a word of Spanish. For some reason, the pretense was amusing and I never corrected him.

Barbers were another example. They never looked at you directly, but at only your head. They didn't make eye contact, but looked disconcertingly at something above your eyes: your hair. They must have seen thousands of heads every day, black ones and brown ones, curly hair and straight, kinky hair and thin, lank strands. It never seemed to matter whether you just had a haircut or not. They were always open for business. I walked by the same barbershop many times a week in Zamalek and they always sized me up, always gestured to the empty chair no matter how shorn I looked or how many times I had already passed that day. But I had my hair cut for ten pounds in Dokki near the office. The kid knew that I need a two-centimeter trim every month or so and there was no shampoo or attempts at a razor cut. I used to go to Mohammed Junior's in Mohandessin but this was much more convenient.

I never thought much about needing a locksmith. They are the kind of people you never think about until you need them. And then you need them badly. They must see thousands of locks every day, big ones and little ones, padlocks and dead bolts, easy touches and the difficult ones to pick. I needed a locksmith when the shipper delivered our household goods from Niger. Most things were intact but I couldn't find the keys to the glass cabinet portion of the bookshelf. We had the bookshelf made in Pakistan, a copy of a fine English mahogany piece. It sat solidly in place, made of heavy *shisham* like rosewood, almost exuding oil. It wasn't like Egyptian furniture, which looked like it was made of hardwood, but was cheap and soft. This was the real thing. But the upper half, with its glass doors, sat locked and precariously perched on the lower cabinet while I decided what to do next. On the way back from an errand I saw a man in the street with a large ring of keys hanging from his belt—a *miftahgi*, if there was such a thing in colloquial Arabic—and asked him to come up to the apartment with me. Here was a live one, he must have thought, and he agreed at once.

He was filthy and hadn't shaved in days. The ring he carried was about a foot in diameter and he must have had three hundred keys on it—a key for every lock in Cairo, I joked in the elevator. He just grinned. In the apartment he took off his shoes, sat himself down in the middle of a Persian carpet, and set to work. He sized up the situation before turning to that portion of the ring that had the right type of key. He detached a smaller ring of maybe ten keys and tried each one in turn. None of them worked. Then he peered through the crack into what he could see of the lock mechanism and opened the ragged valise he was carrying and took out a little package wrapped in cloth. It was another set of keys of the same type. None of these worked either.

The locks in the cabinet were of brass and sat on either side of a center post, each operating one of the doors. The lost keys were also brass, old fashioned, like skeleton keys. He said they were made in the United States but I told him they were from Pakistan. He just grunted. Then he took out a BIC lighter and used it to look through the crack again. He was sixty-eight, he said, but didn't wear glasses. I needed my reading glasses just to see what he was doing. I had a good view since I was holding the upper cabinet in place. I don't think he understood—although I tried to tell him—that the cabinet, maybe seven feet high, four feet wide and a foot deep with glass doors, was only sitting on the lower portion. Until we opened it and fixed it with the screws, it would sit there precariously. But he kept pulling on the doors as if he didn't understand. I had visions of the whole thing falling on him and the glass cutting him to pieces.

His three-hundred-plus keys didn't include one that worked. So, he decided to make one. Out came something that looked like cheap bottle opener. Then from the valise he took a hacksaw blade and a pair of pliers. With a few deft strokes he cut it to the desired length and then used the pliers to bend it to the right shape. Like all Egyptian craftsmen, he threw everything on the floor. It was for the boy, his *biliya* or apprentice, to follow after him and clean up the mess. There was no boy with him, but the little pieces still flew in every direction. There was something out of the *Arabian Nights* about him: from the rag he wore around his head, to his rheumy eyes, to the nose that perpetually dripped. He worked feverishly, like an afreet or jinni, and paid no attention to what I said. He was preoccupied, with a half grin that played across his face. When he concentrated—like now, where he was feeling with the key he had just made—the grin became wider and I could see that most of his molars were missing. But at sixty-eight it was a wonder that he had any teeth at all.

The new key didn't work either. I asked him if he thought he could open it and he said, distractedly, of course, *as saber gamil*, just be patient. Then he took out the BIC again and tried a new tack. He saw something he liked, because now he took out a small screwdriver with a plastic sheath around the blade, the kind electricians use to check the flow of current. Out of the valise came another pair of pliers and he removed the sheath, the little bits of plastic flying in every direction. He inserted the screwdriver in the crack between the doors and began, feverishly, to turn it. There was a single bolt plate in the center post, held by two screws and he was trying to remove the screws. Periodically, he would take out the BIC and peer inside again. Then more vigorous turns. The he pulled on the doors again. Still, it wouldn't open.

Now he went back to the key he had made. He gave the end another turn with the pliers and inserted it in one of the locks. He gave it a great deal of body English, almost turning over with it. He closed his eyes and you could tell that he was feeling for the tumblers. He was now about half an hour into the job and we didn't seem to be any closer to a solution than when he'd begun. I asked him, again, if he was going to be able to fix it and he just grunted. Out came the pliers again and he took another turn on the end of the bottle opener. Then he inserted it again into the lock in the right door and, looking at the ceiling with that half grin, felt for the tumblers. Suddenly, something gave way and he withdrew the bottle opener and pulled on the door. It opened.

Now he applied himself to the left door, which was probably a mirror image of the other lock. After another few minutes he opened the left door. Then he removed the little brass locks from the inside of each door. He would make keys for them, he said. So, I asked him how much he wanted, first to open the doors and then for the new keys. He mumbled something inaudible so I offered him twenty pounds for the work. That's when the fun began.

He was outraged, absolutely refusing the twenty pounds and saying that he wouldn't take less than forty. He didn't just refuse, he brayed. His voice had a strained urgency about it, and he was beside himself with agitation and rage. He turned and twisted, inconsolable. Luiz, the Sudanese houseboy, came from the kitchen where he was ironing and tried to reason with him. He told me he would handle it, but even his "let's be reasonable about this" manner didn't work. Foam flecked at the corners of the *miftahgi's* mouth. Luiz said there was a sick woman next door and that he had to lower his voice. That worked for about a sentence. After another minute of the braying I had had enough and told him that he was through. He said he would go to the police. I said go ahead. Then, he said he would accept an additional ten pounds for the work and so I gave him the thirty pounds.

In the elevator his demeanor changed completely. He was back to his old elfin self, with that half grin splayed across his face. He smiled beatifically at me all twenty-eight floors to the ground and, having gotten what he wanted, he sauntered triumphantly out of the building. He knew all the *bawwabs* and greeted each one in turn:

"Izzayak ya Khairy? Izzay sahitak?"

"Sabah el-khair, ya Hassanein."

"As-salaam aleykum ya Mahmud."

Like all Egyptians he enjoyed a good *dawsha*, or confrontation. It had all been a show. Another *khawaga* taken to the cleaners, although for the equivalent of nine dollars I had received value for money. I eventually found the spare set of keys to the cabinet.

A few days later on Ramses Street I noticed an undertaker's storefront. In front was a hearse, a black 1950s Chevrolet panel truck with a cross and the name *Antoine* in white on the side. Undertakers must see thousands of potential customers every day, black ones and white ones, tall ones and short ones, fat ones and thin ones . . .

8

The Car

An American car is often an albatross overseas. Before it leaves the United States it has already become a problem. The first thing an American must do is remove the catalytic converter since unleaded gas is often unavailable in the developing world. That requires written permission from the EPA in Washington. It also requires reinstallation if the car is to be re-imported to the United States. Then, after mandatory fumigation in Germany, the car will remain in the port of entry, incurring heavy charges for wharfage or demurrage, until the catalytic converter is reinstalled and the car tested for emissions. Assuming years of running on leaded gas has not made it unfit to operate on American roads, it will be certified and readmitted. But it is a lengthy and expensive ordeal.

And that is just the end of the process. The beginning is just as arduous. There are many hurdles to be negotiated before the car is usable overseas. The first is shipping and even if the car is strapped in a container, there is always incidental damage: broken mirrors, flat tires, not to mention batteries and other parts of the electrical system that fail after three months at sea or in port. The port is always a potential problem, with damage or pilfering while the container sits on the pier. Then, there is registration in the new country. Fixers or drivers generally handle this part of the process, including shepherding the car through the inspection process.

Most cars on the streets in Cairo wouldn't pass even an Egyptian inspection, with broken taillights, turn signals, and mirrors, holed mufflers, and emission systems that hardly deserved the term *systems*. The fact that they ran at all meant a combination of the judicious payment of bak-sheesh—otherwise known as bribes—and administrative overload. There simply aren't enough inspectors or hours in the day to make the inspection regime work. We worried not because our cars wouldn't pass inspection but because a foreigner—a *khawaga* in Egypt—was always seen as a soft touch. His shipment will be rifled at customs, routine courier pouches opened, and contents taken. Given the opportunity, the bureaucrats at the local equivalents of customs or the DMV—the *mugamma'* or the *mourour* or the *gamarik*—would make his life as difficult as possible.

We generally relied on others to deal with the bureaucrats. I was advised by one driver not to speak Arabic when the presence of the *khawaga* was required. "It will be better for the full respect," he insisted. So, I stood mute while we were ushered with five *fellaheen* into the presence of an officer in the traffic department. He was uniformed, with four stars on his epaulets, and sipped tea while we cattle stood dumbly in his presence. The driver pleaded my cause with considerable unctuousness and we were dismissed with a snort and a wave of the hand. The dependency on drivers led to abuses of its own. We knew that they made a little extra on the transactions by overstating the costs of the license fee, of copying official documents, plasticizing the license, paying baksheesh, etc. The amounts were petty and the drivers may have needed the money, but they were already paid more than general managers in the public sector clients we worked with. And the baksheesh was corrupting. But somehow the system worked. When I returned to Egypt in 1995, a clerk in the traffic department in Cairo retrieved my file from the archives. It was a dusty folder, six inches thick with all my old licenses from 1980 through 1985, each having required a new application and a new form every six months when the work permit was renewed.

There were a few advantages to having a car overseas. Gas was generally cheap, ranging from the equivalent of about a dollar per gallon in Egypt to about half that in Saudi Arabia. Repairs could be inexpensive. Local mechanics were notorious for their ingenuity, being capable of repairs that Mr. Goodwrench had long since forgotten. They had to be ingenious to keep the motley collection of vehicles on third-world streets in operation.

It wasn't always inexpensive, though. Parts for an American car often had to be imported and that meant either a long wait or customs duties, or both. And while the repairs kept the car in operation, they did just that until the next problem arose. Preventive maintenance, like preventive dentistry, was unknown in most third-world countries. When a tooth abscessed it was pulled and some of the repairs were the equivalent of an extraction. Cars took a terrible beating, especially in Cairo where the streets were narrow and the tolerances were measured in millimeters. In three years in Egypt the Blazer was hit five times—always while parked—and I stopped counting the number of side view mirrors, at seventy-seven dollars a copy, that were snapped off.

Insurance was expensive since the car had to be insured for its full dutiable value. That meant at least twice the value when new, even with an older car. Most cars in Cairo probably were not insured, but a *khawaga* who did not insure himself was asking for trouble. In fact, the customs duty was our greatest problem. Since the cars were imported duty free, at the end of an assignment we had to sell them, reexport them, or pay the duty. For an older car the duty would be many times its street value. Sometimes the only alternative was driving a car to Alexandria, putting it on a ferry and pushing it into the Mediterranean while underway. Duty-free status required a letter from a sponsor agreeing to pay the duty if the foreigner reneged. It was always difficult to transfer ownership, especially with an older car. So, the American was often unable to sell the car to another privileged person. He couldn't reexport it since the car probably no longer met American emission-control or other safety standards. And he couldn't leave the country without disposing of it. The Mediterranean was the only answer.

There was another alternative and it was not a pleasant one. In the eighties in Egypt we bought a new Niva, a Russian four-wheel drive vehicle, duty free. It was actually a Fiat and was ideal for bouncing around Sinai. Like a Kalashnikov, it was simple, had few moving parts, and was reliable as long as Ivan had been sober when he machined the heads. At the end of the assignment, we spent three months looking for another privileged person to buy it. We thought we had a buyer until the Canadian Embassy refused to issue the required letter, even though the car had only eleven thousand kilometers on the odometer. It was almost brand new.

There was no question of exporting it, even to Europe which was now beginning to enforce standards for safety glass, antilock brakes, etc. So, we "donated" it to the Customs department. The registration had expired while we were negotiating the terms, so we were charged for the registration— and a penalty—before the gift was accepted. It had been Martha's car and she took loving care of it, even giving it a name. In a few weeks it would look like the other wrecks on the road. It had cost only a little over four thousand dollars so the loss wasn't that great. But it nearly killed Martha to see her baby driven away.

The duty-free allowance was designed to allow expatriates to bring in vehicles for their private use. But we were not allowed to profit from the sale of the vehicle, assuming a sale was possible. Any profit had to be remitted to USAID. It was a system that cried out for abuse and it was abused. In 1996 we heard that six US Embassy direct hires had been fired for using duty-free privileges to bring in cars for Egyptians. They were only the ones who were caught, and there were surely others who were not.

In Egypt, the vehicle of choice was the Mercedes, the bigger the better, although big BMWs were making inroads into the upper end of the market. Our dentist, a trim, calculating little man, thought a Mercedes was just too flashy. He drove a "BM" and so did his wife. Together, with duty, they probably cost over £1 million, or $300,000. In the Arab world a man wasn't really a man until he had a family, and that meant a big car. I could count on the fingers of one hand the number of sports cars—that vehicle of the unmarried, narcissistic, Western male—that I saw in ten years in Egypt. But everything else was available.

There were Fiats and Seats and Nassers, the local version assembled in Egypt. From Japan there were Toyotas, Mitsubishis, Suzukis, Nissans, Datsuns, and Mazdas. Ladas and Nivas came from Russia, and from Europe came Opels, Fords, Renaults, Citroens, and Peugeot 504 station wagons, the village taxis of Upper Egypt. There were also Hyundais, KIAs, Hondas, Hiaces, Zastavas, Ibizas, Daiwoos, and some oddballs: Dacias and Atekos from Romania and Skodas from Yugoslavia. There were only a few Volvos, Volkswagens, and Range Rovers, the last advertised as "the best four-by-four by far." Not if it was the product of British technology. There were even a few newcomers: crazy-looking, brightly-colored, top-heavy little things called Atos or Terios or Matiz.

The model names were odd. The Japanese and Korean cars had names that sounded Italian, things like Laganza, Ethino, Corsa, Vitara, Felicia, Elantra, and Vectra. When Viagra first appeared in Egypt everyone thought it was a new Japanese car. But the Italian cars—the Fiats, of which there seemed to be an endless number of models—had names like Dogan and Sahin. As Russel Baker had famously noted, the days were long gone when cars had names that described real things, like "Falcons" or "Eagles."

American cars were largely represented by the Jeep Cherokee—pronounced *che-RO-kee*—assembled in Egypt. With Egyptian labor costs a

fraction of those in the United States, there should have been savings on lo-
cally-assembled models. But customs duties on the imported components
meant that the same car was cheaper in the United States. American sedans
never really caught on in Egypt. There was an occasional Mercury or a new
Chevrolet Caprice—maybe the ugliest car on the road—and a few Lincoln
Town Cars. The Town Car was like a small ship and may have worked in
some towns, but not in this one. American cars often had customs plates
from places like Nuweiba' or Safaga indicating that they had been brought
in by Saudis or Gulf Arabs. There were a few Cadillacs. I once saw an older
green Cadillac in the back seat of which sat a corpulent, heavily-jowled
figure smoking a cigar. He was a caricature of a capitalist and was, in fact,
Fuad Serrag ed-Din, the head of the Wafd, the old party of privilege in
Egypt.

They said that an assembly plant in Egypt needed a least one hundred
thousand units a year to break even. But even though no one was close to
that number, all the big manufacturers were assembling vehicles in Egypt.
They must have been after market share. The small truck market was especially attractive, given the need of Egyptian farmers to move their produce
to market. So, there were Ramses, little S-10 Chevrolets, Tatas, Toyotas, Suzukis, Daihatsus, and Isuzus. Even Bedford assembled a little truck, not the
bulbous, brightly-colored things that we remembered from Pakistan. The
sport-utility craze had also reached Egypt and there were Fords, Hummers,
Blazers, Land Rovers, Mitsubishis, Musos, Toyotas, KIAs, Range Rovers,
Nissans, Mercedes, Fronteras, Suzukis, and, of course, Jeeps.

Spare parts for this menagerie were a problem but the Egyptians had
solved it with their usual ingenuity. In Bulaq there was the spare parts *suq*.
It was a warren of little shops and men smoking *shishas*, like the *sha'bi*
Cairo butcheries. But instead of the cows' heads and sheep's feet, livers,
duodenums, chitterlings, glistening pink lungs and windpipes, there hung
auto parts. There were tail pipes, differentials, axles, grills, steering wheels,
mirrors, seats, headlights, chrome strips, and all the parts that made up the
internal combustion engine. If you wanted Fiat parts, there was the Fiat
man, or several Fiat men. If you wanted Mercedes, there was the Mercedes
man. Most makes were there and you paid less than on Champolion Street
where the shops were more reputable or on the Alexandria road where the
dealers were located. The dealers had computerized parts lists. But there
you had to put up with "the parts man," an officious bureaucrat the world

over. It made a trip to the car dealer as unpleasant as any, the post office not excepted.

Driving was a constant adventure, but not as intimidating as it first looked. After a while you adjusted. Egyptian drivers were actually very forgiving, shrugging off offenses that in Los Angeles would be shooting matters. The Egyptians thought they were the best drivers in the world, not surprising since they thought that they were the best at everything else as well. It did take ingenuity to drive in Cairo and if everyone behaved like Germans the city would soon be in total gridlock. In the early eighties on a visit to Cairo, the humorless chairman of Arthur D. Little opined that he had never before seen people honking at a red light, as if that would make it green. I said that I had never seen anyone in Cairo *stop* at a red light. He was not amused.

Cairo traffic flowed everywhere, like water. If there was an open lane it immediately filled, even though there was a car double parked fifty feet ahead, blocking the lane. They'd sort out that problem fifty feet later. Perhaps it was a congenital inability to plan ahead. Egyptians were famous for filling both lanes of traffic, in the same direction, on a two-way street. Driving the wrong way on a one-way street was, of course, a mere peccadillo. There was the joke that in Germany, everything was forbidden except what was expressly permitted by law; in France, everything was permitted except what was expressly forbidden by law; in Italy, everything was permitted especially what was expressly forbidden by law. Egypt was like Italy. But it could be dangerous. I remembered one Ramadan, seeing a Mercedes approaching at speed, at dusk, on the wrong side of a divided highway. It was simpler than finding an exit and going the right way.

Another favorite was turning right from the far-left lane, or vice versa, across several lanes of traffic. There was the story of the Egyptian driver who did this on a freeway, dodging other cars as they hurtled up behind him and then passed. An American passenger asked what the hell he was doing. The driver said that he was just making a turn. And, by the way, he had his turn signal on. "But it was the left one," said the American. "Well, the other one didn't work" was the reply.

The latest plague was the mobile telephone. If driving a German car had been a status symbol in the eighties, driving a Mercedes or a BMW and talking on a cell phone at the same time was the new status symbol in Cairo.

Traffic police in Cairo were, for the most part, ornamental. They were generally kids from the Delta or Upper Egypt—*felaheen* or *sa'ida'*—who were doing their alternative military service. But the military got the smart ones. One of these kids would be in the middle of a street trying to direct traffic, with no one paying the slightest attention to him. He had a little pad on which he was supposed to take down the license numbers of the cars that were guilty of infractions. That was how the system worked. At the end of the year, when you renewed the car registration, they would total the infractions and assess the fines. But I have seen a cop struggle with pen and paper, even assuming he was literate and could remember the tag number, before the malefactor disappeared in a cloud of diesel exhaust. It was hopeless.

In Cairo, at least, you couldn't build up much speed. In Jeddah it was not uncommon to see big American cars running red lights at 60 mph, with the occasional carnage that ensued. We knew the American who ran the General Motors dealership—the Chevrolet Caprice was the car of choice in the peninsula—and he always took photographs of the remains of other cars after an accident with one of those American monsters. I remembered the picture of a BMW broadsided by a Caprice and reduced to eighteen inches between the doors on the driver and passenger sides. The Saudi driver was still there, compressed into the eighteen inches. The Mecca road was like the Autobahn and no one paid attention to the speed limit. It was not uncommon to be passed, on the shoulder, by a car traveling so fast that it hardly had time to appear in the rearview mirror.

Pakistan was just as bad, except that they always drove on the wrong side of the road. There, the vehicle of choice was the Mitsubishi Pajero. Pakistani drivers had the same odd set of driving skills as the Egyptians. The headlights weren't generally turned on, even at night. It ran down the battery, they said. Cars maneuvered in a perpetual gloom and only when he saw a vehicle approaching did a Pakistani driver flash the headlights, generally blinding the other driver with the high beams. During the day, the flashing headlights had another meaning: "Here I come and you'd better get out of the way."

The turn signals were another favorite. They were sometimes used to indicate direction. But since everybody did what they wanted anyway, the turn signal took on another meaning. A right turn signal meant "I am not turning left." The emergency flasher meant "slow down because I am slowing down," or even "I am going straight ahead." It was perfectly logical: there were signals to tell when you were going left or right, why not one when you were going straight ahead? Mirrors were useless since what was behind you did not exist. If you merged, without looking, into stream of traffic, well, that was someone else's problem.

But the horn was the ultimate favorite. You could be blind and drive in Cairo but you couldn't be deaf. In fact, the horn was the most important part of the car. It was used as an almost involuntary reflex. I once counted the number of times a taxi driver tapped the horn on a mile-and-a-half drive to the office. I stopped counting at thirty-three, even though it was early in the morning and there was almost no traffic on the street. One of the early Arthur D. Little consultants concluded that the horn was used to establish an envelope of space around the car. It was just the kind of thing a consultant would say. But armed with his horn, a Cairo driver could do whatever he—or she—wanted. The women drivers were just as bad as the men.

There were no women drivers in Saudi Arabia, although they had organized a kind of protest—a caravan of female-driven cars through Riyadh—during the Gulf War. The Saudis were about to give women the license in 1979, just before the siege of the mosque in Mecca. But they brought in French and Jordanian special forces to clean out the snipers and that was too much for the ulama. Women drivers would have to wait. We sometimes drove the causeway to Bahrain and it was always a sea change from Saudi Arabia. The Saudi police were unpleasant little men, whippet-thin like Bedouins, although some had a protruding belly and steatopygia, giving them an inverted S shape. The Bahraini police were all British spit and polish. But the greatest shock on the island was nearly being run down by a Bahraini woman driving a Mercedes.

The first thing that Cairo pedestrians—in general, a nimble bunch— discovered was that a vehicle always had the right of way. It was a little like the rules of the road at sea: there were burdened vessels and privileged vessels and, under maritime law, the burdened vessel had to maneuver to avoid a collision. The privileged vessel could not maneuver except in extremis. As long as everyone understood the rules, the system worked. It was like that in Cairo. A pedestrian knew that he was always burdened and had to maneuver, and did so with little hand signals that the drivers understood. The problems occurred when the rules were violated, like someone stopping for a pregnant woman weaving her way through a stream of traffic with a small child in tow. That was dangerous because no one knew what the driver was doing. And then there was the deference paid to technology: the walker gave right of way to the automobile.

In Cairo there were too many people in the streets and too many cars on the sidewalks. But there were other occupants of both the streets and the sidewalks: bicycles and motorcycles, often with sidecars; donkey carts and mule carts, dissimilar animals often yoked together; horse-drawn wagons with fellaheen bringing mounds of cabbages or cauliflower to market; horse-drawn carriages like the *tongas* in Pakistan; flocks of goats and fat-tailed sheep, the latter marked with spray paint and waddling off to their rendezvous with the halal butcher; and herds of camels at the end of their long journey via Darb al-'Arba'een from the Sudan. The 'Arba'een was the forty-day track from Kordofan to Assiut, and the animals were on their way to the camel market at Imbaba.

But behind the jokes and the antics of Cairo drivers there lay a grim reality: Egypt had the highest accident rate in the world. There were only a few million cars in the country of sixty million. In 1998, the English-language *Al-Ahram Weekly* reported, there had been over twenty-two thousand road accidents in which more than five thousand people had been killed and twenty-three thousand wounded. That sounded like war and it was. Egypt was, quite simply, the most dangerous place to drive on the planet.

My problem in March 1999 was a breakdown on the road to 6th of October City. I was going to a new golf course, one of several that were springing up around Cairo. The golf courses had introduced a new kind of vehicle to Egypt: the golf cart. Now, armies of Asian gentlemen, mainly Koreans and Japanese, motored over undulating, wind-swept dunes carpeted with Bermuda grass. The Dreamland course was first rate, 7,400 yards from the back tees, difficult trap placements with real sand, and large, lightning-fast greens with water hazards. When the wind was blowing—and since the course was new, there were no trees to knock it down—it was almost impossible to score. It was not the kind of golf I was used to in Egypt.

In the eighties golf had been the only clean, green thing to do in Cairo. The best course had been at the Mena House, an old royal hunting lodge turned into a hotel. It was really only a nine-hole course with alternating tees to make up the eighteen. There were, of course, no carts. We walked with caddies who sometimes found a lost ball when they weren't trying to hustle us for a few pounds. The groundskeepers sold the lost balls to the next foursome. The course lay under the pyramid of Cheops, probably the most exotic setting for a golf course in the world. By now I had graduated from the old persimmon driver to the new metal woods, as I had to if I still wanted to be longest off the tee. What the hell good was playing golf if you couldn't be longest off the tee? But I was still enough of a Luddite to believe that you should walk a golf course. So, I literally ran the 7,400 yards after the others in the foursome who rode in shaded comfort from hole to hole. At the end I was wind-burnt, sun-burnt, foot-sore, exhausted, and frustrated. Worse, the Blazer had broken down a few miles short of Dreamland and, on the way back, we stopped to see if it was any better after a few hours of rest. It was not. So, I had called one of the company drivers that afternoon and we agreed to retrieve the car the next morning.

Saber met me at the office at 9:00 a.m. He had come in his taxi, a Hyundai. It was good, he said, but not strong. I had my toolbox and we took a company van. The van was another crazy story. Since this was a government project we had to buy American vehicles and they were always difficult to maintain. This car was a Ford and we had to replace fuel-injection parts the year before. But we discovered that although the body was a Ford, the engine was a Nissan and the parts had to come from Tokyo. The van sat in the shop for three months, other parts deteriorating, while we waited for the new splatters. So much for "buy American." It was a reminder of the city of Los Angeles in the Japan-bashing days, canceling an order for rapid-transit cars from Japan. Then they discovered that the American cars had more Japanese content than the Japanese cars.

Named after the outbreak of the Ramadan War, 6th of October City was one of the satellite cities that was supposed to take the pressure off Cairo. The road—through desert with deposits of gypsum on either side— was serviceable. By the time we reached the Blazer, forty-five minutes from Dokki, it looked just as we had left it the afternoon before. But closer inspection revealed that the passenger window had been shattered. Little bits of glass covered the ground and the inside of the car. But the thieves had taken nothing of value. Theft and violent crime were rare in Egypt. The stereo was still there, and so was the spare tire. The glove compartment had been rifled, but it had only the owner's manual and a few miscellaneous receipts. But the thieves had, maliciously, wrenched off the driver's side-view mirror. It was a molded plastic part and the broken mirror would be of no use to anyone.

Saber started to fiddle with the battery. But then he found that there was no fuel in the carburetor, although the tank showed half full. There was clearly a problem in the fuel line and we decided to tow it back to Giza, about five miles away. Saber set to work in his usual matter-of-fact way. He understood how to do almost anything with his hands. He was a typical Egyptian with an extended family that could provide any service an expatriate needed. When I had copper cooking pots retinned, he said he had a cousin who worked with metals and could have done it for less. So, I gave him a brass mirror and asked him to clean it up. It came back beautifully silver plated.

Saber found a long strand of barbed wire, doubled it, and attached it to the towing hitch in the back of the van. I didn't think it was strong enough but he said it was. Then he played out the thirty feet to the Blazer, found a purchase near the riding arm on the driver's side and attached it. He was nicely dressed in clean Levi's, a chambray shirt, and tasseled loafers. He had recently married a very pretty young woman and she was, of course, pregnant. She would probably drop her first child nine months from the wedding night. But the difference today was that she would probably have only two. One of our older drivers had ten children, although only five had survived. Saber lay on the floor mat from the Blazer while he attached the wire. His wife would give him hell if he got the Levi's dirty.

He took up the slack in the van, I took my place behind the wheel in the Blazer, the wire went taut, and we began our odyssey. We bumped along the right shoulder for two hundred yards until Saber saw a *fetha*—a break in the center strip—where we could turn around and head back toward Giza. But the problem was that he slightly overshot it and made a sharp turn to the left. Now I was still on the right shoulder, he was in the left lane, and thirty feet of doubled barbed wire was strung out over the surface of the road. This was a divided highway and cars and trucks that had looked tiny in the rearview mirror were approaching at an alarming rate of speed. We waved frantically and they slowed just enough to bump over the wire before hurtling off to 6th of October City.

This clearly wouldn't do. So, Saber returned to the right shoulder and together we stroked our chins. That's when the second problem arose. We had stopped across the road from a prison and the alarm bells had gone off. An officer hurried across the road and, with a perfunctory hello to me in English, told Saber that we couldn't stay there. Saber asked him what he expected us to do. The officer didn't know or care but we had to move. So, we bumped another two hundred yards down the shoulder to another *fetha*. This time we made it across and turned slowly onto the opposite shoulder. At least now we were both headed in the right direction.

But this was not going to work. The wire broke twice in the next mile, and we parked while Saber went over the hill to a village to find a rope, or *habl*. He came back after half an hour with fifty feet of nylon rope about half an inch in diameter. But even that broke, repeatedly. It was almost impossible for the two cars to move at the same time and the sudden tension snapped the rope. Surprisingly, we had no trouble with the police. We were stopped at several checkpoints—they were probably looking for Islamists on the way into the city. These cops were not kids. They were for real and could be capricious. But they examined Saber's papers and waved me through, rope and all, without stopping.

The last time it broke we were one hundred yards from an Esso service station. So, Saber made a final repair on the rope—now reduced to several ragged strands—and we struggled into the station. I asked the station manager if we could leave the car and bring our own mechanic. He said yes, and that we should park it under the "umbrella." That meant the shed. Saber, of course, knew of a mechanic and an electrician nearby. The battery had failed while we tried to start the car and he insisted we needed both men. They were probably cousins.

Nearby meant ten miles away off Feisal Street, parallel to Pyramids Road. Feisal Street may have been wide, but we soon entered a warren full of children, street dogs, and the usual urban squalor of Cairo. The lanes were festooned with what looked like metal chaff and little tin lanterns left over from Ramadan. There was barely enough room for the van to maneuver. But we eventually found the Engineering Workshop for Automobile Repairs. That was typical Arabic syntax, and we were used to seeing signs like Ibrahim for Keys or Mahmoud for Food Sufficiency. Saber greeted them like the old friends they probably were and after a few minutes Ahmed and Salah joined us in the van. Neither was much over twenty and they came with the usual inadequate set of tools. But Ahmed, the mechanic, showed his mettle when we got back to the car.

He crawled under the Blazer and quickly discovered the problem, a blockage in the fuel line just below the engine. He called for a wrench calibrated in *boosa*, or inches. Fortunately, the right open-end wrench was in my tool box and he set to work. The station attendants—I counted ten of them, all kids and all dressed in their red Esso uniforms with ball caps—watched and smoked. No one could make a decent ball cap except Americans or Chinese and the brims of the caps drooped sadly. Gas station attendants in Egypt were paid nothing and relied on tips. A pound—about thirty cents—was the standard tip and a man could make a decent living with enough traffic. Downtown, there were convenience stores in the big stations, where they sold auto accessories, junk food, stuffed animals, and plastic toys. There may have been commissions. But it was all imported from the United States and I don't know who bought the stuff.

After about fifteen minutes Ahmed emerged from under the car, covered to the elbows in oil and grease. We maneuvered the two cars into a kind of mating position, jumped the battery, and primed the carburetor. On a signal I turned over the ignition and the Blazer sprang to life. Now the fun began.

I asked Ahmed how much he wanted.

"*Zai ma inta aiz*, whatever you want," he said.

That was the standard opening gambit.

"*La, inta aiz kam*? Come on, how much do you want?"

I knew he had an opening number but he didn't want to say it.

He licked his lips and finished wiping his hands. He was just a kid and had only a few scraggly hairs on his chin and upper lip. He was thinking. He had Salah to consider. And then there would be Saber's cut of the take.

"*Sabai'een guinea*."

There. Seventy pounds was the opening bid. But we both knew it was too much.

"*La'a. Ihna hina fi Amrika ow Almaniya*? Come on, where do you think we are, in America or Germany?"

So, we went back and forth and eventually settled on fifty pounds. I gave ten pounds to Salah who had fiddled with the left directional light to make himself useful. So, for a total of sixty pounds, or about eighteen dollars, I had fixed the problem. All parties to the transaction left happy. I drove back to the office where I would leave the car in the garage until the glass was replaced. I paid Saber another sixty pounds for his overtime and ten pounds for the rope.

The insurance company repaired the damage without a police report. S-10 windows were available since they assembled the truck in Egypt. The mirror would take longer. But they were cooperative if you were a *khawaga* with a fleet of company vehicles. The East Company for Insurance had even replaced the cracked windshield from Pakistan. Khaled, our office manager, told them to fix it if they wanted our business, and they did.

Maintaining a car in Egypt wasn't easy or inexpensive. Registration and insurance would together cost about $800 a year. Even the cost of shipping the car was taxable income to an expatriate before a change in the tax law in the midnineties. Cars took a terrible beating in Cairo and I had already replaced a clutch, brake shoes, the side-view mirrors, and an antenna. The gas was often bad and took a toll on the fuel system. The total was probably over $1,500 a year when all the costs were added. And that wasn't even counting the customs liability. Other consultants used company cars, for which they were charged a small monthly fee. But they didn't have as much fun as I did.

I eventually sold the Blazer to an engineer who wanted the car for his farm in the Delta. He was probably no more an engineer than a mujahideen commander in Afghanistan had been a doctor. But the Afghan had taken a six-month course in first aid in Peshawar and would forever be "Dr. Mohammed." In Egypt anyone who worked with his hands was an engineer, or *mohandis*. Better yet, he was a *bash mohandis*. At any rate, the sale was the usual mild aggravation. There were multiple trips to USAID, to ARENTO, to the customs department in Nasr City, and the *mourour*, or DMV, in Dokki. The car had been in Egypt long enough to qualify for duty-free status, but the paperwork necessary to erase the liability was still considerable.

There were forms to fill, letters to write, baksheesh to pay, and passports to be stamped. The one positive in the process was that the new vice chairman of finance at ARENTO was computer literate and quickly signed the release letter I brought to his secretary on a diskette. A step that normally would have taken days was completed in a few minutes. The gritty details were handled by our fixers. The engineer had his fixer and I had mine, one of the drivers from the office. I paid my man and assumed that he would pay his. But after money had changed hands and the sale was consummated the other little man followed me down the street in Dokki, literally pawing at me for his share of the take.

When it was all over it was with a sense of relief that I had gotten rid of the car and the liability. But it was also with a tinge of regret. The Blazer may not have been the best car we ever owned, 1985 not having been a very good year for Chevrolet. But for all its superficial flaws, the engine was strong and had never failed us. And the car was a veteran, having survived campaigns in the high Sierra in California, the lower Himalayas and Karakorams in Pakistan, the Sahel in West Africa, the Sinai, and the oases in the Western Desert of Egypt. In a few months on the farm it would probably look like Martha's Niva. But it was a trooper and would probably survive that campaign as well.

9

America in Egypt

IN THE MIDNINETIES THE American Embassy said that there were fourteen thousand to sixteen thousand Americans in Egypt. Americans overseas come in several types. There is the middle-aged, ecotourist-couple type, striding purposefully through the Marriott, the man in Levis and a safari hat and carrying a backpack. His mate strides beside him, wearing a commonsense skirt or Levis ensemble and no makeup. They are looking for an ethnic group to empathize with, although Arabs don't really seem to count to them. It would be impossible to measure their capacity for goodwill, for understanding the point of view of the other man. It has reached the point that they have no point of view of their own.

Then, there are the innocents who come to work abroad in their middle age. They are appalled at the filth of Egypt, even in Ma'adi, before they settle down to a kind of tolerance while they do their bit for the country. As long as there are bacon cheeseburgers available on Road 9 they are happy, although life is a constant trial. It is a matter of duty, although USAID makes the duty less onerous than it might otherwise be. Their driver becomes their window on the world, their translator, money changer, financial advisor, commercial intermediary, and, in some cases, surrogate husband. The driver, of course, has an extended family and stable of acquaintances capable of supplying everything the expatriate wants. Some Americans even want to take him back to the United States when they leave. The driver, wanting a green card like everyone else in the developing world, has no idea how difficult it will be for a man with rudimentary language skills to find a place in America.

The availability of food in Egypt has improved dramatically since the eighties. Then, there were shortages of things like sugar or ketchup or mayonnaise. We actually became very good at making our own mayonnaise; all you needed was a blender with a drip feed, oil, an egg, and a few spices. We actually thought our tarragon mayonnaise was better than anything in the store. Now there is plenty of mayonnaise, good Dijon mustard, horseradish, and countless other little delicacies. But they are expensive, maybe twice what you would pay for them at a Safeway in the United States.

Americans, not being ones to take this kind of thing lying down, organized a scheme for buying food in bulk and shipping it to Egypt duty free. It was a kind of precursor to Costco. Then you could get things like a case of Hellmann's mayonnaise at wholesale prices, a great savings. None of us was going broke living in Egypt. But if each of the Americans in Egypt spent $1,000 per month—on food, entertainment, essentials, and nonessentials from the Khan el-Khalili—we were collectively dropping $80 million a year on the local economy. That was in addition to the government aid. I don't think Americans begrudged the local merchants the cost, but it was the idea of the thing that grated. It was like paying Telecom Egypt rates for calling the family when callback was available at a fraction of the price.

The bulk-buy system was run by a steely housewife in Ma'adi, which made it useless to someone who lived in the city. The trip down the Corniche was a full day's work, even if you had the time to understand the arrangements. It worked by the purchase of a container of dry goods from the United States. Beforehand they circulated a catalogue with more than four hundred pages of groceries, cosmetics, over-the-counter medications, and sundries. It included twenty-five pages devoted to pets. The section on pets showed how different the United States was from almost every other country on the planet. Here we were in a country of appalling filth and poverty, where the animals in the Cairo Zoo were probably better housed than most humans in the city. The *zabaleen* who collected Cairo garbage ate what they could, fed what they couldn't to the pigs, and recycled almost everything else. But Americans, consumers of 25 percent of the world's energy, would be bringing in things like the Ultra Mouse cat toy, hamster and gerbil food, Yummy Bone hock bones, the Mad Mad Tug dog toy, the Love Your Dog shampoo, the Kaytee Bird suet rack, and the Scoop Away scented kitty litter.

As contractors, we would periodically gather in USAID and discuss our performance. "We" had achieved 25 percent GDP growth, said the functionaries, having reengineered themselves into a system of what were called *performance indicators*. But the real question was how much influence or leverage we really had. The Egyptians were going to do things their own way, as might be expected of the citizens of a sovereign nation. United States policy was not popular in Egypt and we were always a potential embarrassment to Mubarak. He made helpful noises about the peace process and the prime minister made helpful noises in the Peoples' Assembly about the need for reform. But Egypt was still a desperately poor country, and the economic reforms that had taken place seemed disproportionately to benefit the entrepreneurial or just the new wealthy class.

The reforms were not popular except with those who stood to benefit directly from them. There were local subcontractors who knew the rules better than the American firms they worked for and had become used to the gravy train. The selling off of the country's assets at ten cents on the dollar, or ten piasters on the pound, seemed to be the way most developing countries privatized. But it was hard to understand why anyone would want some of the old leviathans like the Helwan Iron and Steel works or the Naga Hammadi Aluminum smelting plant. With the GATT and the WTO, even a domestic market for the output did not seem assured.

The Peoples' Assembly—according to law made up of 50 percent workers and farmers—was the scene of raucous debates on privatization that touched on sovereignty and protection of the disadvantaged. Not that it was really democratic. The democracy was a sham, stage managed to ensure the overwhelming representation of Mubarak's NDP. Everyone said that if the elections were really free the NDP would finish a poor third to the Muslim Brotherhood and the New Wafd. Instead, if the government wanted a bill to pass, it would pass. But there was a considerable amount of venting, letting off steam, that took place in the Assembly. It was there that the allegation was seriously made that USAID's investment in the sewage systems in Cairo and Alexandria was designed to prevent the use of the untreated water to grow wheat and so compete with American wheat on the world market!

Of all the American investments in infrastructure, the sewers seemed to provide the most obvious benefit. Anyone who had seen children in poor residential areas of Cairo, like Sikakini or Old Cairo, puddle hopping in gray sewer water would have welcomed the new systems. But if the Peoples'

Assembly could find a reason to object to the sewers, imagine the reaction to privatizing the telecommunications system. Here we were talking about the crown jewel of the country, a license to print money, with security and sovereignty issues attached. If the multinationals came in, so the story went, Egypt's telecommunications system would become the plaything of foreign agencies, with conversations and data carried by means of arrays of low earth-orbit satellites, with software to allow the CIA to monitor every conversation in Egypt.

But they had partners in their conspiracy theories. A paper by an American academic would occasionally appear, suggesting that American agricultural assistance had only weaned Egyptians from their reliance on agricultural-based protein in favor of animal protein. Traditionally, Egyptians ate beans, *fool*, and they weren't known as *abu zirt*—or the father of farts—for nothing. *Fool* and *ta'amia* were still the filling and inexpensive staples of the poor, but they were eating more meat per capita than ever before. Egyptians increasingly fed grains to animals instead of eating the grains themselves. They then ate the animals, just like Americans did. So, they now relied on wheat imported from America to feed themselves. This was fair enough. But then the paper seemed to go off the rails. It was all part of a giant plot and if the export of wheat to Egypt ended, the entire agricultural price-support system in the United States would collapse.

At 185 kilograms per capita per year, Egyptians were the largest consumers of wheat in the world. Like in the old Soviet Union, subsidized bread was probably so inexpensive that it was thrown away or fed to the animals. The word for bread in Egypt, *'eish*, meant the same thing as "life, livelihood, subsistence," and that was a measure of its importance. The price had been ratcheted up recently, although the attempt by Sadat to increase the price of bread in the seventies had produced riots in which scores died. The *'eish baladi*, or country bread you bought in the streets today, wasn't very good. And the *'eish shami*, or "white bread," was like the pita bread we bought in the States, bland and tasteless. But good *baladi* was available—for a price— in the streets, and all the big hotels now had a *forn*, or oven, on-site and a plump *fellaha* to make their own. Egyptian food was really very good, and the big hotels were now unashamedly serving the best of it: *molokhea* and rabbit, fish *tagen*, *neefa* or steamed goat, along with the standard kabobs and *kufta*. French food was still featured at the expensive eateries, but it was marginal. But they knew how to do good Egyptian food.

Political reform was a difficult issue in Egypt. Americans were certainly aware that this staunch supporter of our efforts in the Middle East was a managed democracy, more managed than democratic. But several considerations stood in the way of our insisting on meaningful political reform along with the economic reform. In the first place, the constitution was a socialist one and privatization was, technically, unconstitutional. But no one wanted to touch the constitution, lest the Islamists become involved and, from a socialist state attempt to make it an Islamic one. In the second place, there was the Islamist problem itself that the regime had controlled through draconian security measures. The Islamists had been driven out of Cairo, although there were supposed to be pockets remaining around the old Fatimid city. They were now in Upper Egypt, hiding in the fields around el-Minia and Mallawi and occasionally ambushing police and killing Copts. There were tens of thousands behind bars on the mere suspicion of Islamist sympathy, but no American administration would dream of requiring that the regime loosen its grip. Egypt was no Algeria, in spite of Luxor. But if there was anything the rest of the world could agree on it was the need to contain the Islamism. It had replaced Communism as the great American bugbear.

Iran had shown the emptiness of the Islamist agenda but that didn't mean that there weren't others anxious to make the experiment. In the occupied territories we are quite willing to overlook, even encourage, the excesses of Arafat's security apparatus, even though we find him undemocratic when he does our bidding against the Islamists. Actually, it was the Israelis who first fostered the growth of Hamas as a counterweight to the PLO. The Islamist threat is only the wrong-headed cry by the long-suffering poor in the Arab world who have been left behind by, first, the socialist apparatchiks and now by the crony capitalists.

Islam was great in the heat of its pristine manifestation, seems to be the idea, and it will be great again if only Muslims revert to the practices and dress of that age. It is attractive to many and it is not difficult to see why. The Islamists were first on the scene after the earthquake in 1992 in Cairo, with their networks of self help. The government showed up much later. The same is true of Hamas in the occupied territories. During the political campaigns in Egypt the religious parties—although not necessarily Islamist—marched in great serpentine masses through the poor neighborhoods of Cairo chanting, "*Islam, huwa'l-hal, Islam, huwa'l-hal.*" "Islam is the solution," they said. Given the poverty and hopelessness of Egypt's poor, it would be difficult to argue with them.

Religion or nationality or xenophobia or fear carries everything else before it, including gender. Women are as prone to reject the advice of outsiders as the men, even when the outsiders are pushing gender issues. The sisters must wonder why the greatest resistance to Western calls for an end to female circumcision is from African women themselves? Women are the ones wearing Islamic dress—the simple wimple among the more liberal, the full regalia, including veil and gloves, among the more conservative. Maybe their husbands or fathers or brothers put them up to it, but I'm not so sure. And it isn't only with Muslims. In an interview, a Russian pop singer spoke about the solidarity of the Slavic brothers and the Orthodox people. She didn't mention the Slavic sisters. The Slavic brothers have shown in Bosnia and Ingeshutia and Chechnya and Kosovo just how violent and brutal they could be.

Even the Copts are not interested in being tarred with the brush of being outsiders. It is certain that they chafe under the restrictions imposed by the government. But when the World Council of Churches lists Egypt as one of the countries where freedom of religion is under threat, their immediate reaction is to close ranks with their Muslim brothers. They are not interested in any more trouble than they already have. Democracy is a many-edged sword.

Giving free play to political opinion in Egypt would create more problems for America than it would solve. That is because there are as many unreformed and unrepentant Nasserists as there are Islamists out there, and a reading of representative sampling of the Arabic newspapers on a daily basis would reveal how inconvenient other peoples' ideas can be. These opinions are not tolerated in any real sense by the regime, although people are permitted to vent and the opinions have a kind of nuisance value. The peace treaty with Israel, always unpopular, is doubly so now with Netanyahu in power. He is aggressive and particularly nasty. Stick your finger in the Arabs' eye whenever you can, and if you can find that one eye is more sensitive than the other, stick your finger in *that* one. He takes particular pleasure in humiliating the Palestinians. That is not lost on the nay-sayers who always said this peace wouldn't work in the first place.

10

Day Trips

Suez

September 14

SUEZ WAS A BIT of a blank in our knowledge of Egypt. We had passed it many times, often before sunrise to ensure an early start in Sinai. There seemed little reason to stop. Niebuhr had described it as a squalid little town in the autumn of 1763,[1] but there were things of interest in the vicinity. I wanted to see if there was anything left of Kulsum, the Greek city of Clysma, or of the canal that once ran to Cairo from the vicinity of that city. And then there was 'Agrud, about eleven miles short of Suez, a famous watering place that marked the beginning of the wilderness or, coming from the east, the sown. Both Niebuhr in the eighteenth and Edward Robinson in the nineteenth century left detailed descriptions of the journey from Cairo to Suez, with a catalogue of *wadis*, plains, and *jebels*.[2] They illustrated the difference between hurtling over the highway at 70 mph and the more leisurely pace of a camel. But there was also the ability to recognize geological and geographical features at a glance, and the painstaking habit of mind that it required.

I left after dawn this time and made a point of looking for interesting features in what had always been a boring and featureless prelude to the spectacular vistas of Sinai. But there was little to see other than the brooding

1. Niebuhr, *Travels Through Arabia*, 175–77.
2. Niebuhr, *Travels Through Arabia*; and Robinson, *Biblical Researches in Palestine*.

presence of the range to the south, Robinson's Jebel 'Atakah, an extension of the Mokattam east of Cairo. I had last been in Suez in 1980, when several of us drove through the city on the way to 'Ain Sukna and the beaches on the Gulf. It didn't leave much of an impression then. This time, instead of turning off to the Ahmed Hamdy tunnel, about fifteen miles short of Suez, I continued on to the east and the city. Suez announced itself by several refineries, including the Nasr Oil Production Company, NAPCO, where the road came to an end. There was a choice of routes: north to the city or south to 'Ain Sukna.

I decided on the city first, even though the range to the south had grown closer and higher, and it now loomed across a spit that connected with the Gulf. The city was nondescript, and I drove as far east as I could before reaching the water. At the edge of the canal there was a radar tower and, beneath it, a white pedestal about twenty feet high and ten feet on a side, covered with graffiti. I asked several boys whose statue had once been there, but they confused the words *timsal*, or statue, with *timsah*, or crocodile, and also with the name of the lake to the north of Ismai'liya. Finally, one blurted out that the pedestal had originally been part of a monument to Ferdinand de Lesseps, the French developer of the canal, but that the statue had been pulled down during the war of independence in 1956. Then they told me that in the same little paved area overlooking the canal there had once been two lions—they debated the difference in Arabic between lion and tiger—whose empty pedestals they also pointed out.

I asked them about Kulsum and they said that it still existed, and was in the 'Arba'een area to the north of the city. So, I drove back the way I had come, but turned north, and soon found myself outside the city and moving parallel to what looked like the canal. I stopped and walked fifty yards before climbing a berm. It was the canal, with navigation buoys and moorings looking like they hadn't been used in years. So, I asked a man cutting brush by the side of the road and he said that 'Arba'een was back the way I had come. I should take the right fork at a *midan*, a roundabout, the left going to Port Tawfik. After several more stops for directions, I found myself in a little area of shops where Shari'a tel Kulsum was supposed to be.

Sure enough, a street sign in Arabic bore the name. A barber told me it was all that was left of tel Kulsum, the mound itself having been leveled years ago, along with the Jewish *madafin*, or tombs, near the town. The tel had once been noticeable, but everything had been built up over the years and was now changed. This area was no longer part of Suez proper. It was typical Egyptian urban squalor, with garbage in the streets and the carcass of dog growing fat and grinning in one pile. The people were friendly, but they were poor and generally dirty, with bad eyes and bad teeth. And, unusual for Egypt, they looked undernourished.

There were a few graceful old buildings with wooden latticed balconies like those in Port Said. But they were abandoned and a crew was dismantling one, piece by piece. There was a plain little mosque next to a tile factory, with an octagonal minaret made of wood laid horizontally and then plastered over. It was abandoned and dilapidated. Only a part of the large municipal headquarters building was being used as a police station. The remainder was abandoned, with the shutters falling off the windows. Of the canal that once came here from Cairo, nobody knew anything. Like so many attempted forays into the Egyptian past, this had been abortive.

On the return to Cairo I turned off eleven miles outside of Suez, where the map showed 'Ajrud to be. Almost everything on the road from Cairo to Suez was controlled by the military, and this was no exception. The railroad, half a mile north of and parallel to the road, was blocked by a gate but a military policeman in the little shed next to the tracks said there were *athar*, or ruins, nearby, and they raised the gates and let me through. He got into the car and came with me. We turned east on the other side of the tracks and ran parallel to them for a couple of hundred yards, before we turned south again and parked in a swale. The top of what looked like a fragment of wall showed on the other side of the tracks and down a slope. From the crest, we saw a crew of maybe fifteen men with wheelbarrows working at the site.

They were from the Egyptian Antiquities Organization and showed me around. Little remained above the hills except the wall fragment. But they had excavated the circular pit of the well, lined with very regular sandstone blocks. It was about ten feet in diameter and, the man in charge said, about one hundred feet deep. There were several other structures under excavation, including a bath perhaps fifteen feet by twenty feet and three feet deep, and a pit forty by forty feet and ten feet deep, which was used to water the animals. The sides of the latter were lined with brick, graduated backward from the bottom to the top at about ten degrees from the perpendicular. There was also the remnant of a circular tower that looked like one of the *burgs*, or towers, in the Fatimid walls of Cairo. This was the *qal'a*, or fort, and there had been other facilities nearby.

The man showing me around said that this was the last place the pilgrims stopped in Egypt on their way into Sinai, and the first place on their return. Niebuhr said the fort was completely fallen down in 1762 when he stopped there, but that potable water was available.[3] He was reminded of Num 33:6:

> And they departed from Suc'coth, and pitched in E'-tham, which *is* in the edge of the wilderness.

And Exod 13:20:

> And they took their journey from Suc'coth, and encamped in E'-tham, in the edge of the wilderness.

In 1816, J. L. Burckhardt spent three days inside the walls to avoid being plundered by Bedouins. Robinson and his party only had a glimpse of 'Ajrud, "a square fortress with a well of bitter water two hundred and fifty feet deep, built for accommodation and protection of pilgrims on their way to and from Mecca."[4]

One of the soldiers wanted a ride back to Cairo and I took him along. He was bright and it seemed that his father had been an ARENTO switch manager during the eighties. He pointed out a few things of interest, including Jebel 'Aweibid to the north of the road, and the cemetery for Egyptians lost in the '73 war. It was at the sixty-kilometer post from Cairo, where General Ariel Sharon, commanding officer of the Israeli army, halted his incursion in 1973. I knew that since I was keeping a close watch on the odometer. The distance from the refinery at Suez to the underpass as we entered Cairo was seventy miles. Robinson reckoned "somewhat less than seventy-five statute miles"[5] from the eastern gate of Cairo to Suez. Niebuhr had calculated it at thirty-two leagues.[6] At 2.3 English miles to a German league—a figure I had previously calculated—his total would be just over seventy-five miles. It was close enough.

---

3. Niebuhr, *Travels Through Arabia*, 173–74.

4. Robinson, *Biblical Researches*, 1:65.

5. Robinson, *Biblical Researches*, 1:66.

6. Niebuhr, *Travels Through Arabia*, 174.

Dahshur

October 6

In keeping with our resolve to see more of Egypt this time, I decided to visit Dahshur. Laura and I had driven past it on our way to Maidum a couple of months before. I had called the American Research Center and they said we needed a pass that was available at an office in Giza during the week. But then I spoke with someone at the British Embassy and she said that we didn't need a pass. So, I decided to chance it; it was only an hour and a half south anyway and it was a pretty drive. The weather had broken and it was now cool. I invited Grant and Josie along, as they never seemed to get very far off their spot on the West Bank, as Grant called it. They were, as usual, good company, Grant with a quip for every occasion and Josie rising, like a fish to the bait, to a discussion of every serious subject. Grant was an American who had been overseas for most of his working life but had managed to avoid infection with any of the languages he had encountered along the way. Josie was born in the Netherlands and had the verbal facility that seemed to characterize the Dutch. She had lived through the war and the German occupation and spoke of the sound of the V-2s overhead as they streaked toward London from Peenemunde.

As a young woman, she had worked as a chambermaid in Paris, walking up the spiral staircase to the garret where she lived in that characteristic Paris apartment configuration. She later spent several years at sea as a translator with P&O Cruises. Her English had a particularly Dutch lilt to it: things were "guude" or "baad." And they were always one or the other with Josie, never anything in between. And she took no prisoners. Once, she had blasted a hairdresser at Mohammed Junior's for cutting her hair too short. The man probably hasn't recovered yet. Mohammed Junior was the odd translation of *Mohammed Soghair*, odd since there is no concept of "junior" in Arabic. It was the smartest place in town in Cairo and the weight of gold in the women's salon on a given day would probably have retired half the national debt of Egypt.

When I picked them up that morning Josie showed me the new calico cat she had found in the street. It was a kitten weighing eight ounces, she said, four of the ounces having been added since they found her. All calicos were females, Josie told me. She carried a can of tuna outside and we waited while she fed the strays in a derelict car next to the apartment building. Nearby was the villa owned by Osama bin Laden. On the drive south, I made the same mistake we earlier had with Abusir, another pyramid complex in southern Giza: the pyramids were at the first turnoff, not the second, and we had to make our way back north on the little dirt road inland from the main Saqqara road. At a fork we met Mohammed, a guide licensed, he said, by the Antiquities department, and he rode with us to the asphalt road and the main entrance. Guides were generally an annoyance but this time we were glad he had come along. There was no need for a pass. We drove toward the Red Pyramid, looming up ahead. It had just been opened to the public after years of isolation for "military" reasons. There were a series of steps and then a guardrail leading to the entrance halfway up the face and a few people, looking like ants, were making the ascent.

But first we wanted to see the Bent Pyramid, sitting a mile away to the southeast. So, we drove the mile through the sand and Mohammed moved the rocks blocking the entrance to the parking area. There was no one else there. From the outside, it was even more striking than Maidum. Most of the limestone casing was still intact and there was a very sharp line where the original angle of incline changes to the shallower angle, giving it the bent appearance. The entrance was open, but there were no stairs and no guardrail and the face was very smooth. At Mohammed's suggestion, I climbed about half way up, but I could have fallen and broken an arm or leg or worse. So, I didn't go any further.

We walked the circumference, past the little temple at the end of the causeway coming up from the valley temple, and two large stelas. They were identical to those we had seen at Maidum but broken off about halfway up. Mohammed said a great deal of work had to be done before this pyramid would be ready for visitors, but I was just as glad we were seeing it as it was. We had it entirely to ourselves and it was far more interesting than Giza. With the casing intact, we saw how fine the joinery had been and there were no men on camels or horses to bother us.

We drove back to the Red Pyramid and Grant and I went inside. The descending passage—lighted by a generator since the electrical lines had not yet been connected—was a steep incline, maybe seventy-five yards long and smooth, with only about three feet of headroom. Grant, ten years older than I, labored mightily on the way down. At the bottom, there was a little bridge and then the first of three chambers, articulated in three-foot sections to a kind of Gothic ceiling. I counted thirteen sections. Another bridge took us to a second, identical chamber, and then a series of stairs and platforms to the main chamber that must have been twenty feet above the other two. They were all of what looked like black granite or basalt, very finely fitted together.

Grant always came prepared, wearing a Swiss army knife even in the office in a little leather pouch on his belt. Here he had a flashlight, and in the first chamber we saw writing on the underside of the first section. It was graffiti, done in fine block letters, and we could just make out the names Kirwan, Gliddon, and Hopley and the date 1836. I later read in Robinson's *Biblical Researches in Palestine* that G. R. Gliddon was the American Consul in Cairo when Robinson passed through the city in 1838.[7]

Outside, but still at the top, we paused and gave our thigh muscles a rest, the long descent and then ascent in a crouching position having given those muscles a particular workout. At the bottom Josie was waiting for us. She wanted to know what it was like inside and Grant said that he didn't know, having spent most of his time trying to catch his breath. I told her about the three chambers and, when she asked who was buried there, Grant said, "Kirwan, Gliddon, and Hopley." We agreed that the visit had been a great success and Mohammed accepted ten pounds gratefully.

On the drive back to Cairo we got into some heavy discussions of the veil, female circumcision, medical care in the developing world, and general male perfidy. Josie was sitting in the back seat but leaning forward between the two front seats and making points by stabbing with her index finger. After about ten minutes of this I suggested that we change the subject lest it interfere with the safe operation of the vehicle, as they would say at the DMV. The Dutch are people of strong opinions.

Friday was Grant's day at the British Club, where he could put down a few pints then sleep it off at home. They also exchanged VHS tapes for new ones at the library there. The club was posted with examples of British humor and Grant was always in search of a joke. Many were of the infantile sort, and typical was a poster of a flasher in the men's room with the caption "Expose yourself to Ireland."

Tel el-Yahudiya

October 11

The Royal Danish expedition to Happy Arabia represented a milestone in European understanding of the Arab world. But, though it had advanced

---

7. Robinson, *Biblical Researches*, 2:547n2.

secular knowledge of the Arabs, it had a fundamentally religious purpose. The foremost Middle-Eastern philologist in Europe, Johann David Michaelis of Gottingen, had conceived the notion of sending a group of scholars to the Yemen where, he understood, an eastern dialect of Arabic closest to Hebrew was still spoken. This, he believed, would advance European knowledge of the Hebrew Bible. The expedition was delayed in Egypt for over a year in 1761–62, and this accounts for the prominent place Egypt occupies in Niebuhr's *Travels in Arabia*.

Given the frame of reference, Niebuhr interested himself in anything having to do with the Jews. To the north of Cairo near present-day Shebin el-Qanater there is a ruin called Tel el-Yahudiya, or "mound of the Jews." I decided on the spur of the moment on a Friday morning to look for it and Grant was anxious to go along. I put off buying gas until we were out of Cairo and could ask directions with a better chance of getting something accurate.

So, we drove north past Bulaq and the World Trade Center and stopped after a few miles at an Esso station. The attendants all crowded around if only to hear the *khawaga* speaking Arabic, and one was from the Shebin el-Qanater area. It was his country he said, but we drew a blank when we mentioned Tel el-Yahudiya. Finally, he said that what we were looking for was really Tel Beni Temim, of which Tel el-Yahudiya was a part. It was the first of many bits of misinformation we were to receive that day.

Shebin el-Qanater was about twenty-five kilometers further north and that was the simple part. After about fifteen kilometers a policeman turned us around and sent us to the right, over "the second railroad crossing" where a railroad guard confirmed that the town was thirteen kilometers straight ahead: "*Ay awamir, ya Basha*. Any assistance you need." Short of the town we asked directions again and were told that Tel Beni Temim was three kilometers ahead, and to the left. A second *fellah* confirmed the information and, sure enough, there was a sign with "Tel Beni Temim" in Arabic pointing to a little dirt road leading to the left from the main road. We drove down the dirt road, past *fellaheen* with loaded donkeys and camels, until we came to a dead end in the squalid little town. A one-eyed vegetable seller sitting on his donkey cart told us, with obvious impatience, that this was Tel Beni Temim, but that there were no *athar* or ruins here.

He gestured broadly and said that Tel el-Yahudiya was back in the direction we had come. But he said there were no ruins there either, it all being *taht el-miya*, or inundated. So, we retraced our way and before reaching the main road we asked a young man in western dress where the mound of the Jews was. He said he knew and was going in that direction himself so we took him along. His name was Ashraf. We returned to the main road but crossed it, turning this time to the right, and drove a few kilometers through fields of cotton, *fool*, rice, and citrus trees. Then we entered another little town and crossed the canal where we dropped Ashraf. Ahead of us he said, after a few kilometers, was what we were looking for. And so it was. Five minutes later, looming yellow at a height of about fifty feet out of the green fields, were the ruins.

The site was large, over twenty hectares according to the plan I had seen in the *Atlas of Ancient Egypt*.[8] The highest mound covered the ruins of the town and the second, to the northwest, the ruins of Leontopolis, built by the High Priest Onias in the second century BC with the permission of Ptolemy VI Philometor. Niebuhr had been right in his conjecture. It was excavated by Naville in 1887 and more thoroughly—needless to say—by Flinders Petrie in November of 1905. Petrie had to deal with standing water and a plague of mosquitoes, as well as flocks of sheep driven across the ruins at night. In fact, the mounds had already been plundered by *sebbakheen*, farmers, looking for fertilizer for their fields.

Petrie confirmed that the temple of Onias was patterned on the temple in Jerusalem and that, based on the design of the perimeter glacis and the names on scarabs, the main mound should be attributed to the Hyksos. There was still standing water and we had to skirt it to make the ascent. We climbed to the top of the first hill and then down a swale to the second, a lower series of mounds. The area was covered with shards and thorn bushes and individual mud bricks were identifiable in some of the walls. But aside from a broken woman's shoe and—appropriately—the jawbone of an ass, we found nothing of interest. We were apparently of interest, however. The sight of the crazy *khawagas* climbing over these barren heaps was beyond the comprehension of most passersby.

We drove back through agricultural scenes typical of the Delta. The fields were carefully tended but the canals, where everyone washed themselves, their clothes, and their dishes, drank, defecated, and threw the occasional dead animal, were open sewers. We even saw some of the old 1940s and 1950s taxis, Fords and Chrysler products with the engines removed and diesel engines installed in their place. We hurtled back into Cairo on the Cairo-Alexandria agricultural road but soon encountered gridlock

8. Baines and Malek, *Atlas of Ancient Egypt*, 174.

somewhere near Shubra. It took us nearly as long to reach Ramses street as it had taken to reach Shubra from Shebin, with several more instances of conflicting directions. Our sense of relief as we drove up the 6th of October Bridge was palpable.

II

Miscellaneous

The Egyptian Museum

TODAY I VISITED THE Egyptian Museum. I was, again, on the trail of Niebuhr and looking for stelae taken from Serabit el-Khadem in the early part of the century and a black granite sarcophagus he had seen in the city in 1762. I didn't find the sarcophagus I was looking for, but three very much like it and the tale is worth telling. On one of the three, with the same inlaid decorative motifs but slightly different hieroglyphs, there was an Arabic catalogue number. So, I asked a young woman in the office on the first floor what the number meant. She led me into the bowels of the museum where a young man named Adil told me that the number I had seen was not the one I wanted. But if we went back and looked together we might find it. Sure enough, a small number in English, in red—No. 29302—was on the top of the sarcophagus and that was the key. So, we returned and entered an office where eight immensely fat women sat, eating pastries.

With ill grace one of the women brushed aside the crumbs and allowed Adil to open her desk where he found a long ledger, looking like the accounting books in ARENTO. In the ledger was a listing of the numbers and we scanned them until we found 29302. Next to it was a picture that identified it as late Persian or Ptolemaic. However, that was only step one. We would have to wait for Mustafa who had the key to the bookshelf we needed to continue the process. He would be there in five minutes, said

Adil, who then disappeared. Now, in Egypt "five minutes" really meant nothing except that Mustafa wasn't there and probably wouldn't come that day. Sure enough, Mustafa didn't come and Adil never returned. But much longer than five minutes later someone else did. We found 29302 in a chart on the wall which identified it as having been catalogued by Maspero in 1914 and we would find it in catalogue forty-eight. And there it was, in volume forty-eight of the *Catalogue General des Antiquities Egyptiennes*, fully described in French with a reading of the hieroglyphics.

I didn't see Niebuhr's sarcophagus that day and, in fact, I later found it in the British Museum. But I did learn enough to know where it had come from—certainly Saqqara—and what it might have represented. I also found one stela from Sinai. But the visit was interesting for another reason: they were beginning to build a computer database in the museum. A couple of young women sat in the room where I was reading and reviewed the codes from a handbook—a separate number for an arm, two arms, leg, trunk, torso, etc.—before laconically entering them in the database. The general complaint about the Egyptian Museum was that the exhibits were not properly displayed and catalogued. But it looked like all the information was there. It was just a matter of making it available to the public. Someone suggested that it was purposely withheld to give scope to the rogues who lead tour groups through the museum. I resisted the impulse to be righteous on the subject since I had seen Martha that morning as I meandered among the catafalques. She was escorting a group of American ladies through the exhibits on the first floor.

We passed like ships in the night.

Luiz

In Cairo we shared Luiz, the Sudanese cleaner, with Grant and Josie. In spite of the fact that Grant had spent most of his working life abroad, in places like Iran, Iraq, and Saudi Arabia, he was hopeless with languages. Josie, like most Dutch, was not and had spent many years at sea with P&O Cruises as a translator. But neither of them could get "Luiz" right, and he was "Looie" to them. His full name was Louis Augustino Laku Lado, and he was not an Arabized Sudanese from Khartoum, but a Central African Christian from Juba, one hundred miles north of the Ugandan border. He was probably a Dinka like Manute Bol, and was just as dark and thin, but not quite as tall. I gave him my old Pierre Cardin blazer and he would arrive in the morning looking very smart. The four-inch lapels were even coming back into fashion.

Luiz was very methodical, much better than an Egyptian maid. The floors were immaculate, the windows sparkled, and the apartment could have passed a US Navy dust test. He even made us inspect what he had done. But we eventually had to restrain his use of water in the bathrooms: it was so profligate that the particleboard of the cabinet doors began to de-laminate. Like Richard, our housekeeper in Niger, he ironed beautifully and the only thing we didn't ask him to do was cook. But he had his own way of doing and could not be broken of certain habits. Grant forbade him to enter his computer room, drawing an imaginary line on the floor and telling him not to cross it. But day after day of looking at the computer excited some irresistible urge in Luiz and he entered the room just to dust the table, he said. But he had to move the computer in order to dust, dropped and broke the printer and so confused the series of wires, cables, and power strips that it blew out the main power supply.

Tears followed and Grant was as angry as Grant could be, which was not very angry. Luiz also dropped an expensive pottery lamp in our apart-ment and the tears again flowed freely. Grant greeted me the other day with a cheery, "Well, he got 'em. Two at one blow." Luiz had dropped two of his prized pint beer mugs brought from England and shattered them both. We kept him, though, because he really was priceless. One thing puzzled me, though: like Richard in Niger, after he dusted the pictures they all hung cockeyed, not just a little bit out of plumb, but at crazy angles. He didn't seem to see the problem. Someone suggested that it was to let us know that he had dusted them, and that may have been the answer. He showed a great deal of initiative and we didn't discourage it. When he pulled the face off one of the drawers in the kitchen, he took out my tool kit and repaired it. I didn't object too strenuously to the smiles he left in the drawer face with the hammer.

We probably paid him too much, and Grant and Josie surely did. Josie, for all of her toughness, had no sense of proportion and would pay a taxi driver twenty pounds for a three-pound ride. She said it was to avoid trouble, but it had the effect of making trouble for everyone else. We even negotiated a weekly food allowance for Luiz and, although I thought it was too much, we still paid it. It wouldn't be fair to change the rules in the middle of the game. The combined salaries were double what we paid the drivers in the office and half again the salary of the manager of cost accounting in ARENTO. That little man had a family to feed. But maybe Luiz did too. Like most Africans he probably had an extended family, some in Juba, some in a squalid refugee camp in the Sudan, and the odd brother in Cairo. And Luiz probably brought home the bacon for them all.

So, we didn't begrudge him the money. But then he began arriving in the morning in new pants and *docksiders* for chrissakes. They were like those things advertised in the L.L. Bean catalogue as "Moose Mocs" or "Trapper Mocs," with the "Comfort-Core system for cushioning and a sturdy outsole for street wear." Combined with the cotton dockers and blazer, he looked like he had just joined a fraternity. I half expected him to say "bitchin" when I told him to clean the refrigerator. We left him alone in the house; not only would mistrust be corrosive, but we had better things to do. However, I had to admonish him about using the stereo. Once, he allowed as how he would leave when the football game on the television was over. I told him it was over now.

He was often sick and expected the *patron* to provide medicine. In Niger, I brought three large bottles of Excedrin from the United States and when I looked for a tablet I discovered that Richard had taken them all. We found Luiz one day sprawled over the ironing board, inert and holding his head in his hands. He had a headache, and we had to know that he had a headache. He has asked me several times for aspirin but I told him he could find it himself in the pharmacy. It cost next to nothing. That may have been a little breakdown in the caste system but, like with Mohamed in Islamabad, it could be done. There, Mohamed announced that he was a cook/bearer and he didn't do cleaning. We said that he would clean if he wanted the job. We didn't want a female sweeper in the house, as they were notoriously light-fingered. Mohamed accepted the terms and everything worked out.

Like with Richard in Niger, I sometimes had to be severe with Luiz. He took several buses in the morning to reach Dokki from Roxie in Heliopolis, and so I was willing to put up with occasional lateness. But one morning I had to be in the office by 7:45 and I told him that if he hadn't arrived by 7:30, I would leave. So, I gave him an extra five minutes then left. As I drove up Mossadeq street I caught sight of him striding in the direction of the flat.' But I didn't stop, not having time to park the car again, take the *ascenseur* up to the apartment and let him in. Later that morning at the training cen- ter I got a frantic call from the secretary in the office who said that a man speaking terrible Arabic had called several times and wanted to know what to do. She asked me, in true Booz Allen conflict-resolution fashion, how we were going to solve this problem. I told her it wasn't a problem and didn't need a solution. Luiz could go home and next time show up on time.

The Haircut

Haircuts, like almost everything in Cairo except Italian neckties, were inexpensive. A shampoo and cut at Mohammed Junior's was twenty pounds, or about six dollars, and I had my hair cut there regularly. Mohammed Junior was the odd translation of *Mohammed Soghair*, odd since there is no concept of "junior" in Arabic. It just meant "Little Mohammed." One day there was a new barber in the line, an older man who said he had worked in Italy. That was supposed to reassure me, I guess. But his line of questioning had the opposite effect. First, he asked me if I wanted my hair blocked in the back or cut continental style. I said I didn't know but supposed that a block would be fine. Then he asked me if I wanted my sideburns halfway or at the height of my ear, and I said I didn't know but he could see how I wore them now. This was annoying and I told him that I came to the barber for a haircut not an interrogation, and he was supposed to have answers not questions. That was a mistake. Because with a great *swaatch* of the straight razor he amputated my right sideburn.

He didn't just trim it, he *amputated* it halfway up the side of my head. It was gone and in its place a two-inch strip of pale, white skin contrasted very sharply with the tan of my face. I rose out of the seat and let everyone in the salon know that I wanted a different barber. I didn't care *where* he had cut hair before, he was not going to cut *my* hair. After they had calmed me down, someone else gave me the usual two-centimeter trim. It took a couple of weeks for the sideburn to grow out again and I spent the time walking around feeling slightly lopsided. Frankly, I now think I wore them too long. The Italian-trained barber was later transferred from Mohandessin to the main facility in the Semiramis Hotel. I went back the next time feeling a little sheepish but the other barbers let me know with a wink that they had been amused by the whole incident. Egyptians always enjoyed a good *daowsha* or dustup. But no one would touch my sideburns.

The Resume

A resume is typically an introduction and list of qualifications by an applicant for a position in business. It can be critical as it is often the only thing a potential employer sees, ideally an entree to the next stage in the hiring process. Well prepared, a resume can be the first step in a successful job search. Poorly prepared it is often a ticket to oblivion. If anyone doubted the importance of religion in the day-to-day life of the average Egyptian Muslim, or of attitudes that would seem to fly in the face of Western business practice, the following resume should remove that doubt. It is my translation from the Arabic.

In the Name of God, the Merciful, the Compassionate

Now then:

This interview at the Research Center for the Application of the Islamic Sharia' with Professor Consultant . . . may God bless it and make it beneficial. . . . Amen.

We begin the interview with a resume submitted to the reader of this review.

In the Name of God, the Merciful, the Compassionate, thanks be to God, the Lord of the two Worlds, may God bless and keep our Lord Mohammed, and all of his company . . .

My name is . . ., my father: . . ., the family name: . . . All certificates, papers, and documents attesting to my primary and secondary education . . . are without my father's name, but this includes it.

I was born in 1920 (my age is seventy-one years), and I am blessed with good health. . . . Amen.

I studied at the normal primary and secondary schools. There were no preparatory schools. I graduated from the Faculty of Law at the University of Cairo, the only university in the Kingdom of Egypt in 1942. I made my name working in the legal profession, and was appointed deputy prosecutor, as graduates generally were. I thus began my practice of the law. I worked as a deputy and continued my studies and in the practice of the law. After a period as a deputy prosecutor, I moved to the court of first instance and then to the appellate court. I ultimately became Chief Justice of the Appellate Court of Cairo. I retired in 1981. During this period, I was sentenced to imprisonment from 1965 to 1970. The court over which I presided and where I had tried cases, hypocritically had the audacity to condemn me. I entered detention, indifferent as to whether I was sentenced to one, five, or ten years. These were all the same to me, and none was preferable. I persevered and after

> emerging from detention I challenged the court for errors in its decision. After the period of suspension, I agreed to work in legal affairs in the Kingdom of Saudi Arabia until I reached retirement age, although I was still capable of work—officially—until the day of sixty-five years arrived and the decision to retire was taken.

It isn't clear whether he got the job.

The Yakkht Club

Yacht is one of those English words that native Arabic speakers find difficult to pronounce. That isn't because they can't form the sounds, but because written English is not always a reliable guide to pronunciation. In Arabic, at least in the classical language, what is written is always pronounced. Several Arabic letters are not pronounced in everyday speech, but that isn't because people don't know how to pronounce them correctly, but because it is easier not to. Written Arabic, always assuming the word is originally an Arabic word, is an infallible guide to pronunciation. But English is full of words borrowed from other languages, spelled according to the language of their origin. So, an English dictionary will have a guide to pronunciation, with odd combinations of letters and diacritics to represent shades of sound.

The word *yacht* is a good example of a borrowed word. It is pronounced "yot" by an English speaker, and the dictionary renders the indeterminate vowel by an *a* with two dots above it. The *ch* is not pronounced. The word is probably Dutch in origin, spelled originally with a *j* as in *jaghte*. The guttural may have once been pronounced, as it is in the name *Van Gogh*. We pronounce it "Van Go," but to a Dutchman it is something like "Van Gogg." To an Arabic speaker, the *ch* in *yacht* indicates the sound represented by the Arabic *kha*, and they gather spittle when they pronounce it. The word becomes "yakkht," sounding like something in Russian or Hebrew. We can be thankful that it is not spelled with the original *j* because there is no *j*, only a hard *g*, in colloquial Egyptian Arabic. I wouldn't want to guess what it might sound like with a *j*.

I heard the word over and over again in Cairo when we were all taken to the Yakkht Club for lunch one day. It was on the west bank of the Nile but since Shari' en-Nil had become one way, you had to know where to turn to find it. So, there was a great deal of discussion in the car as to the location of the Yakkht Club. And it took us several trips up Giza street—now Shari' Charles de Gaulle—and then back along Nile Street before we found it. By the time we arrived at the club the word *yakkht* had become engraved in Wernicke's area in all of our brains.

It was supposed to be one of the elite eating places in Cairo. We were taken there by a local who, like everyone in Egypt, was of good family and well connected. This was still early in the project and the expats tended to be transported en masse to lunch. When we eventually found the place and the van disgorged the seven of us, the Yakkht Club looked decidedly down at the heels. It was on a barge on the river, outside of which boats were tied up. But if there is one thing that Cairo is not, surprisingly, is a river city. There are few houseboats, no floating markets, no teeming masses plying the turgid waters like Bangkok or Saigon. There are only a few poor fishermen living on the river, families toiling together, the women rowing while the men and boys cast the nets. The occasional marinas in Cairo have a few boats, run down like everything else in the city. This one seemed to have its share of dinghies, a few sailboats, and a few powerboats, but there was hardly a well-maintained one in the bunch.

We settled ourselves and the asked for menus. The Nile lapped at the side of the barge, the surface topped by clusters of water hyacinth. We were the only ones there. The waiter, friendly in an open Egyptian sort of way, was wearing a dirty white shirt with a bow tie and featured a three-day growth of gray beard. It was not designer stubble. The menus were only in Arabic. After translation we ordered and, when the food came, it was typical of the old-style Cairo eateries like Carroll's on Kasr en-Nil street: an odd cut of meat, french-fried potatoes, and a fresh vegetable. You could always tell a Cairo eatery by the french fries. They were large, irregular in size and shape, crisp and hot, not like the thin, soggy things they served at McDonald's. The Yakkht Club was famous for its lemonade and after the expats had carefully fished out the ice cubes, it was refreshing. The mixed grill was the standard fare, consisting of kidney, testicle, *kofta*, and a lamb chop. It was good if unspectacular. The cats thought so too. That was another thing about Cairo eateries. There were cats watching while you ate, cats underfoot, and cats cleaning up the scraps while the waiter cleared the table.

It cost next to nothing and we certainly got value for money. There was even a discussion, on the way out, of how we could join the club if we wanted to. All in all, it was a typical Cairo institution, transplanted to lend the notion to the elite that they were in Europe. It once may have been elegant, although it was hard to see how. But, these days, there wasn't a single yakkht in sight.

Translation

Today the man from the International Office for Translation showed up in the office with my translation, neatly packaged with the bill for E£600 inside. Six weeks earlier I had called the Danish embassy asking about a translation of a portion of *Den Arabiske Rejse 1761–1767*,[9] the book on the Danish expedition I had bought in Copenhagen. I had most of it translated in Islamabad by a man at the Danish embassy and I had even done some of the translation myself. But I couldn't find a Danish-English dictionary in Cairo and besides, I thought someone might want to earn a little extra money. Instead, the embassy had sent me to the International Office for Translation in Heliopolis.

I eventually found their office, but it was a typical example of poor marketing in Egypt. There was no number on the building and I found the office, on the second floor, only after I asked the *bawwab*. The little sign outside the door was only in Arabic. I don't know what people who didn't read Arabic would have done and they, presumably, were the target clientele. There was a single desk in the office and a young woman who spoke very little English. She made copies of the pages I wanted translated. But the door to the room with the copy machine was locked and she had to crawl through a hole in the wall. Then she said someone would call me with the price. It was a total of thirteen pages and, at forty pounds per page—more than we paid in the office for Arabic-English translation—I was prepared to pay E£450–500 for the job.

Several days later Ahmed called. He asked me how I was. I said I was fine. And how was my family? I said they were fine too. Then he said he had examined my work and announced, rather triumphantly, that he would be able to do it for E£1,500. He emphasized the numbers: "One thousand five hundred pounds." I replied that this was outrageous. I told him what we paid in the office and that I was prepared to pay something along those lines. "But," he said, "Danish is a difficult language." I told him that it wasn't difficult for those who knew it, and that was what I was paying him for. So, he agreed to look at it again and call me back.

---

9. Rasmussen, *Den Arabiske Rejse*.

Several weeks later he called me again at home. After the usual formalities he announced that I would be very pleased with his new proposition: he would give me a special price and I would be extremely happy with the product. He would charge me only six hundred pounds for the job. I asked who would do the translation. He said a man who had lived in Denmark for many years. And how was his English? It was excellent, he said. I wanted a copy of the translation on diskette. That would be fine. He would provide a Macintosh diskette along with the hard copy. So, I told him to go ahead. It would require careful attention and I would have to review the product thoroughly before I paid him anything.

Several weeks passed before he called me at home again. He said that he would come the next day with the translation. But he didn't show up. A week later he appeared in the office. The man behind the familiar voice was nicely dressed in a suit and tie, wearing horn-rimmed glasses. His business card was professional looking: "Ahmed . . . General Manager, International Office for Translation." It even listed his cell phone number. But as he spoke I began to wonder if, other than the young woman in the office, he wasn't just a one-man show, because the translation I was looking at had the same fractured flow of his spoken English. In fact, as I told him, it really wasn't English at all.

Most of the words I read were English words but they were in odd combinations, with no recognizable syntax:

> Carsten Niebuhr made gave map of Arabia he was mapmaker. This
> he made map. . .

It was if he had translated the Danish into English word for word, put all the words in a hat, shook it, and listed them as they fell out. It was impossible to understand and I told him, again, that it was not a language that I recognized. Who had done the translation? He said, again, someone who had lived in Denmark for a long time. I said that he may have known Danish but he clearly didn't know English. He promised to correct it. But I told him that even if he corrected the English I would have no assurance that it was an accurate translation of the original Danish. And where was the Macintosh diskette? He promised to bring that too. Then he left.

It was going to be a long time, if ever, before I was "extremely happy with the product." There were several options. The first was a reduced price, and that was the most probable one. Then I would have the translation reviewed by someone who knew both languages. It was a shame, in that here was an example of the entrepreneurship that Egypt badly needed and Cairo was full of foreigners who had translation needs. But being a translator was not an entry-level position. But in the end, I didn't have to exercise any of the options because Ahmed never called again.

12

Books

BOOKS HAVE AN IRRESISTIBLE attraction to the collector, as much for their aesthetic value as for their contents. As repositories of knowledge they have always been important, although that importance has been somewhat diminished with the spread of the internet and e-books. There is hardly a subject one can't find on the web, and in most cases the hard work has been done for us. In fact, many searches result in too much rather than too little information. Wikipedia, a free online encyclopedia, takes a more discriminating view and returns a more scholarly result. But even here there is room for valuing the contributions of encyclopedias. The 1910 eleventh edition of the *Encyclopedia Britannica* is noted for the quality of the authors and travelers cited on the history of the Arabian Peninsula: Hogarth, Niebuhr, Burckhardt, Burton, Palgrave, Doughty, Huber, Nolde, Halevy, Wellsted, and Sprenger, among others. It would be hard to assemble a more knowledgeable company.

But there is another metric that we have yet to speak of: that of the book as an article of beauty, even of art. In the shelves of my bookcase devoted to these same savants, the 1822 *Travels in Syria and the Holy Land* by J. L. Burckhardt stands out for its overall preservation and the quality of its binding. Others of equal provenance on the same shelf, including Niebuhr's *Voyage en Arabie*, published in French in 1780, are of equal beauty. Perhaps surprisingly, T. E. Lawrence's *Seven Pillars of Wisdom* takes the palm, being several hundred years newer and consequently minus the little blemishes that mark the older books. The quality of the Kennington portraits that grace the *Seven Pillars* is especially notable in what was, after all, a trade edition. C. M. Doughty's two-volume *Travels in Arabia Deserta* was also published by Jonathan Cape, with Lawrence's assistance, in 1936. The rest of the glass half of this bookcase is generally taken up with nineteenth-century travel accounts by Burton, Palgrave, Blunt, Hogarth, Bell, Meinertzhagen, and Philby. In addition, there were official accounts of World War I by British (*Mesopotamia Campaign, Military Operations in Egypt and Palestine*) and Australian forces (*Official History of Australia in the War of 1914–1918*), the latter bought in Sidney on a visit in 1989.

The glass half of the second bookcase is, in general, taken up with large works of reference: the 1910 *Encyclopedia Britannica*; Burton's sixteen-volume *Thousand Nights and a Night*; Niebuhr's corpus in German; the *Standard Jewish Encyclopedia*; dictionaries in Arabic, German, French, Turkish, Persian, and *An Egyptian Hieroglyphic Dictionary*. The remainder of the glass case contains books on India and Central Asia. The lower half of both bookcases contains sundry books on Egypt, Pakistan, Central Asia, Arabia, Palestine, and Syria.

It should be seen from this thumbnail sketch that I am a book collector. It is an all-consuming vocation and permits little else when fully at play. Each of the above acquisitions has a story to tell and some of the acquisitions are a function of pure serendipity. On a stopover in Copenhagen, a longer-than-expected wait for a connecting flight meant I had just enough time to make my way downtown to look for bookstores. The first one I found featured the massive tome of Niebuhr's *Den Arabiske Rejse 1761–1767* in the window. I bought it, thereby increasing my carry-on weight by nearly double. But I have never seen it anywhere else. Egypt was a kind of Mecca for a bibliophile if you could put up with the pervasive damp that often compromised the bindings. But rebinding was inexpensive and I have many of these hybrids. Rebinding the Burton sixteen-volume *Nights* in leather and good cloth cost ninety pounds, or about five dollars a volume at the official rate. I still have the set, with my handwritten notes in Arabic in the margins. To a purist, writing in the margins of a book is verboten. But this was an inexpensive reprint, and the value to me of the footnotes far outweighed any consideration of aesthetics.

No one really reads a dictionary for pleasure. You are generally looking for an answer, for a translation. The difficulty of translation varies with the subject matter. I can read most articles on the front page of *Al-Ahram*, the flagship of the Cairo dailies, without a dictionary. Editorials are more difficult and columns—the Arabic equivalents of Tom Friedman or Nicolas Kristof—are more difficult still. This is because of the greater use of colloquial phrases. In a recent column on the coup in Niger I struggled with the words *la yathaqa hata fi sirwal dakhali*. Most were unambiguous, but *sirwal* undeniably meant "drawers, panties," and in one form *la yathaqa* could mean "to unfasten, loosen." I had visions of cross-dressing in the Nigerian military, until one of our translators helped to unravel the meaning: the first form of *wathaqa* meant "to trust" and in this context *sirwal* referred to one's "intimates." In other words, the coup leader couldn't trust his own people. Such are the potential hazards of translation.

I used to read Ahmed Beha' Ed-din's daily column in *Al-Ahram* and, for the above reason, it was always a bit of a struggle. But it was worth it. He was the dean of Egyptian political commentators and, as I recall, a closet Nassarist. There was nothing unusual about that. Egypt was full of unreformed and unrepentant Nassarists. It was the result of the repression by the regime of responsible opposition, which instead became irresponsible and took refuge in old slogans and tired ideas. Beha' Ed-din had been imprisoned with everyone else by Sadat in the early eighties and then banished to the Gulf. He came back in the middle of the decade. I met him at a dinner party given for a buyer for the Library of Congress by the Lebanese owner of one of the better bookstores in town.

He was a little man and as we sat, literally, at his feet I was reminded of Malcolm Muggeridge's description of his aunt and uncle, Beatrice and Sydney Webb. Beatrice was tall and spare and languid, every inch the aristocrat. But Sydney was so short that when he sat in an armchair his feet didn't reach the floor. Ahmed's wife was a redhead and twice his size. He expostulated like a French intellectual and we all listened, rapt (although we had no choice), as he described how the thousands of students at Cairo University, living ten to a room, had once been communists but were increasingly infected by the bacillus of Islamic fundamentalism. That was in 1985. When he died in 1996, the whole country turned out for his funeral.

The mesh of serendipity is exceeding fine. That is what makes book collecting so rewarding. You never know what the next bookstore or next chance meeting in the street might bring. I once met a tiny couple in the Cairo Hilton who asked me to take their picture. They were both in their seventies. He was about five feet tall, wore a beret at a rakish angle, and proudly produced an American passport: "Land of the free and home of the brave," he said. His name was Issaco Ashkenazi and he had owned the best-known carpet store in the Khan-el-Khalili, Ronald Storrs having mentioned it in *Orientations*. He had left on one of the dates that mark recent Egyptian history and was back to see if he couldn't recover some of his lost stock.

His wife's name was Sofia Petrovna Driscoll, the daughter of a Russian shipbuilder in the Netherlands, but previously married to an Irishman. That was the Driscoll part, although he had died of the drink in the Sudan. She had been part of Farouk's inner circle and there is a picture in Artemis Cooper's *Cairo in the War 1939–1945*[10] of the wedding of one Sophie Tarnowska in which the bride looks very familiar. Maybe I got the names wrong. At any rate, my wife and I went to dinner with them in Zamalek. On the way to the restaurant Sophia tripped on one of the execrable Cairo sidewalks and fell flat, although the little thing gamely picked herself up and carried on. During the meal Issaco lapsed into somnolence but she was in her element, telling stories of those long-lost days in Cairo: "And my dear, what a time it was!" We paid the bill.

As I look through the titles on my bookshelves I see a catalogue of names, occasionally recognizable, more often not; that makes them interesting: Meinertzhagen, Storrs, Peake Pasha, Cheesman, Sykes, Philby, Kirkbride, Robinson, Slatin Pasha, Wassmus, Clayton, Hogarth, Wavell, Monroe, Thomas, Antonius, Jafar Pasha Al-Askari, Hitti, Duff-Gordon, de Chair, Glubb, Waterbury, Wilson, Longford, Wingate, Bell, Lorimer, and Lawrence. All have a story to tell, most often told in the first person, which would make them autobiography. Some tell a story about the story, which would make them biography, my preferred genre. Books read in book clubs overwhelmingly seem to be fiction, or novels, where inventiveness is the goal authors seem to be seeking. I prefer the unblemished item and some of the above equal, if they don't exceed, the allure of any work of fiction. They are truly larger than life.

They were bought, most often for a few dollars, not to populate a bibliography of eccentrics, but to contribute to a growing body of knowledge of an area—the Middle East, for all of the imprecision of the term—at a particular time—the late-nineteenth and early-twentieth centuries. Very few were bought from the same seller or bookshop. They are the antithesis of "antiquarian" books, although some are more valuable than others and a few would command a hefty price. It is tempting to think of Olympic boxing-weight classes in this context. There are a few heavyweights in the

10. Cooper, *Cairo in the War*, illustration 32.

above mix, but most are lightweights or welterweights. I have read them all, although I would be hard-pressed to write a synopsis of any one of them at this remove. But I still remember finding Lorimer's 1915 *Gazetteer of the Persian Gulf, Oman, and Central Arabia,* as much for the serendipity that took me to the old Ezbekiyya Gardens before construction of the Opera metro station and relocation of the bookstalls that once almost defined Ezbekiyya. They were now a hundred yards away, near Al-Azhar. The scene was now visually much improved but something about it made me a little sad at their passing.

Lorimer was a member of the Indian Civil Service and it was he who assembled the six dense volumes of text and maps into the above offering. The pervasive damp and humidity of Cairo was exacerbated by the fact that these books were kept outside. Some of the pages were water stained and torn. But if there was anything that Cairo booksellers do well it was re-cover books. So, the six volumes are now resplendent in their new red leather and cloth coverings, their bindings intact. The contents are a vast trove of information, gathered together into volumes and parts, often confusing in their numbering scheme. Sitting cheek by jowl with the Lorimer are the three volumes of Edward Robinson's *Biblical Researches in Palestine, Mount Sinai, and Arabia Petrea.* Robinson, incidentally, is the translator of *A Hebrew and English Lexicon of the Old Testament* (see below).

These books have their own stories for me: where I was when I found them, where I was when I read them, what I was doing when I paid for them. Doughty's *Arabia Deserta* will forever be associated in my mind with Los Angeles where I drove to pick them up. I paid fifty dollars for the two volumes. Gilbert Clayton's *An Arabian Diary* will always bring back memories of Angel Island in San Francisco Bay where I read most of the book. A sudden downpour produced a mud splash that still mars the cover of the book. A note inside the front cover lists the asking price of five dollars. I bought a real heavyweight for forty-five dollars—Gesenius's *A Hebrew and English Lexicon of the Old Testament*—wholly unexpectedly at a religious bookstore in San Francisco. It was the only thing I ever found there. The grass in Peoples' Park in Berkeley was the place where I read much of Sykes's *Orde Wingate.* It was sparkling new and, odd for this group, not used or pre-owned. The published price was forty-five dollars. Philby's *Haroun al Rashid* was notable for the fact that it was hardbound and sold for ten dollars. But there was also most of Philby's extraordinary output, taking up fully half of the shelf: *Arabian Jubilee, The Empty Quarter, Arabia of the Wahhabis, The Heart of Arabia, Arabian Days, Arabia, Sheba's Daughters, Forty Years in the Wilderness, Sa'udi Arabia, Haroun Al Rashid,* and *Arabian Oil Ventures.* What little space that remained was devoted to David Hogarth, Lady Anne Blunt, Gifford Palgrave, and Richard Burton.

The bookshelves themselves are fine pieces of furniture. We bought the first—an old Victorian mahogany piece with glass doors in the upper half—from an antique dealer in Oakland. It was hardwood and heavy, which doesn't appeal to some tastes today. We doubled down in Pakistan by contracting with a furniture maker to make a copy of the Victorian piece according to photos a brother took in California. It was made of *shisham,* or Indian rosewood, and the two together made a handsome pair, each seven feet high, four feet wide, and a foot deep, the second almost as heavy as the first, both almost exuding oil. I made a third, also of mahogany, minus the doors, which largely houses the lesser titles above. Altogether, the three represent nearly eighty cubic feet of substantial space that truly constitutes a repository of inspiration for pieces written but not published.

Disposing of libraries such as the above presents special challenges to the bibliophile. In the first place, the subject matter will be of interest only to a specialist and there are probably specialties within specialties. While this narrows the spectrum, it also expands the knowledge of the prospective buyer. And the internet means that purchase of antiquarian books is not the crapshoot that it once was: careful comparison shopping is now possible where prices, in particular, are posted and can be compared with those of other, identical pieces. But that is not the end of the story. I once paid $1,900 for a 1775 edition of Forskal's *Flora Egyptiaco-Arabica,* which seemed a reasonable price. When the book arrived, I found that it was not bound, and not what I was expecting. In a communication with the seller I learned that some books in this era were sent for binding only on being sold, the owner not hazarding the cost of binding until he had cash in hand. The seller in this case sent me a check for $200, what he estimated would make me whole. The finished product is nicely bound, but clearly not in an original binding.

The internet notwithstanding, an original 1819 edition of Burckhardt's *Travels in Nubia* bought in Cairo was beautiful inside but the binding badly needed work. It was the kind of thing that only visual inspection would reveal. Fortunately, I was in Cairo at the time and was able to fold the cost of the work into the purchase price. The binding strips were hardly noticeable inside the front and back covers. The opposite happened with Lawrence's

Secret Dispatches from Arabia. It was beautifully bound by the Golden Cockerel Press but it was difficult to determine the authorship of some of the contents based, as they were, on unsigned letters from, it was thought, Lawrence. There were also *The Letters of T. E. Lawrence, Revolt in the Desert, The Wilderness of Zin, The Mint, Oriental Assembly,* and Lawrence's translation of *The Odyssey of Homer.* All were a product of the postwar enthusiasm for all things Lawrence and didn't include the real gem of the list, the *Seven Pillars of Wisdom,* in the beautiful original binding. Lawrence was a bookbinder by inclination and the 750 or so printings of the *Seven Pillars,* with the order of the illustrations—different in each one—meant there was no one that constituted a single subscriber's edition. The asking prices ranged widely, from next to nothing to $5,500.

A different kind of a problem presented itself with another reference work, *Webster's New International Dictionary of the English Language,* and all the 3,214 pages and twenty-odd pounds intellectual property that it constituted. I was looking for a definition of *gazetteer.* And there, on page 1,041, I learned that the word could apply to an official appointed to publish the news, or to the news—the geographical dictionary—itself. That was fair enough and answered my need. But there was another metric that applied to this particular dictionary, and it had little to do with intellectual property: sheer physical heft. This book was physically imposing, at twelve inches high, eight inches wide, and six inches deep. That amounted to 576 cubic inches of dense material that had to be accessible to be of use. It meant use of the stairs if, like this one, the book and I were on different floors in the house. The stairs were treacherous for anyone who qualified for membership in AARP, with the handrail critical to maintaining balance. That left a single hand and arm to wrestle with the book. It may sound simple but, in practice, it was daunting and I had visions of slipping or dropping the book, or both. Thank God for *Webster's New World Dictionary.*

Brief Glossary of Arabic Terms

Ablaq	Piebald; a style of building or decoration, consisting of horizontal bands of red stone alternating with white or yellow; sometimes painted
'Aish	Pocket bread, either *baladi* or *shami*
Al-Ahram	Literally "The Pyramids;" name of the flagship of Cairo daily newspapers
'Amm	Literally "uncle;" often applied to older, uneducated men
'Arabiyya	A vehicle; in Egypt, an automobile
Bahri	Literally "riverine;" applied to one branch of the Mamluks
Bakshish	A gratuity
Baladi	Literally "country" as in "country bumpkin;" a kind of coarse pocket bread
Bawwab	A doorkeeper or guardian
Bedu	A Bedouin
Beit	A dwelling, describing a house, apartment, or tent
Birket	A pond, of which there were once several in Cairo
Birseem	Clover, a common fodder for animals in Egypt
Burgi	Literally "of the citadel;" applied to a second branch of the Mamluks
Eid al-Adha,	The Greater Bairam, a feast celebrated during the Hajj
Eid al-Fitr,	The Lesser Bairam, a feast celebrated at the end of Ramadan
Fellah(een)	Farmer or peasant, specifically from the Delta

Fellaha	Female *fellah*
Fool medames	Broad beans, the staple diet of Egypt
Forn	An oven
Gallabaya	An ample gown, often wide-sleeved, worn by *Fellaheen* and *Sa'idis*
Ghutra	See *kufiya*
Goha	A folk hero in Egypt, he often presents as a simple-minded peasant, but is actually cunning and strategic
Hara (Haret)	A neighborhood or quarter in Fatimid Cairo
Hijab	The veil covering the head and neck, not the full face veil; common in Egypt
Iftar	Breakfast, often referring to the meal breaking the fast
Ikhwan	Literally "brothers," often referring to the Muslim Brotherhood
Istiraha	A rest house or inn
Izzayak	"How are you?"
Jebel	A mountain
Karkaday	A refreshing drink made from hibiscus and sold on the streets of Cairo
Khalig	The canal from the Nile that once formed the western boundary of Fatimid Cairo
Khamsin	Literally "fifty," referring to the wind that blows for that many days from the Western Desert in the spring
Khathkuda	An Ottoman military title often assumed by Mamluks; occasionally appears in the vulgar form of *kikhya*
Khawaga	A schoolmaster or pedant, often applied to foreigners
Kufiya	A kerchief worn by peasants, often checked black or red and white
Madrasa	A religious boarding school associated with a mosque
Mamluk	Literally "owned," refers to a caste of white slaves in Egypt

Mashrabiya	Projecting oriel window with a wooden lattice-work enclosure
Masr	The Arabic name of Egypt
Miftahgi	A locksmith
Nabataean	An ancient Arabic people who once occupied northern Arabia and southern Syria; known primarily for the city of Petra
Qarafa	A cemetery
Qarafatain	Dual form of the word referring to the Northern and Southern cemeteries in Cairo
Ra'is	Literally a "chief" or "head;" often a ship's captain
Sabah al-Khair	"Good morning"
Sa'idi	A farmer or peasant, especially from Upper Egypt
Sha'bi	Popular, from "the people"
Shami	Literally "Syrian;" refers to white bread as opposed to *baladi*
Shari'	A street
Shebab	A youth
Shisha	A water pipe
Sufragi	A waiter or steward
Suq	A market
Ta'amia	Bean paste, generally deep fried
Tekiyya	A Sufi hospice
Wadi	A valley
Wafd	The political party called after the delegation that Egypt attempted, unsuccessfully, to send to the peace conference in 1918
Wikala	A caravanserai or rest house
Ya	"Oh," the vocative particle
Zabbal(een)	A garbage collector
Zawiya	A small, informal mosque

Bibliography

Aldington, Richard. *Lawrence of Arabia: A Biographical Enquiry*. London: Collins, 1955.

Baines, John, and Jaromir Malek. *Atlas of Ancient Egypt*. New York: Facts on File, 1980.

Boswell, James. *The Life of Samuel Johnson*. London: Sharpe, 1830. https://archive.org/details/lifeofsamueljohnooboswrich/mode/2up.

Bruun, Bertel, and Sherif Baha el Din. *Common Birds of Egypt*. Cairo: American University in Cairo Press, 1990.

Byrom, John. "Christians, Awake." Hymnary, 1749. https://hymnary.org/text/christians_awake_salute_the_happy_morn.

Church of Scotland Panel on Worship. *The Book of Common Order*. Edinburgh: Saint Andrew, 1994.

Cleveland, John. *The Character of a London Diurnall*. London: 1644. https://archive.org/details/bim_early-english-books-1641–1700_the-character-of-a-londo_cleveland-john_1644_1.

Cooper, Artemis. *Cairo in the War, 1939–1945*. London: Penguin, 1995. https://archive.org/details/cairoinwar1939190000coop/page/n9/mode/2up.

Curtiz, Michael, and William Keighley, dirs. *The Adventures of Robin Hood*. Burbank, CA: Warner Bros Pictures, 1938.

Felline, Federico, dir. *8 1/2*. Italy: Cineriz, 1963.

"The First Nowel the Angel Did Say" [The First Noël]. Hymnary, 1833. https://hymnary.org/text/the_first_nowell_the_angel_did_say.

Flanders, Michael, and Donald Swann. "Pillar to Post." On *And Then We Wrote*, 1975.

Fraser, Antonia. *Cromwell: Our Chief of Men*. London: Arrow, 1997.

"God Rest Ye Merry, Gentlemen." Hymnary, 18th c. https://hymnary.org/text/god_rest_ye_merry_gentlemen.

Guichard, Roger H., Jr. *At the Margins: Four Years in South Asia and West Africa*. Eugene, OR: Wipf & Stock, 2017.

———. *Masr*. Eugene, OR: Wipf & Stock, 2015.

———. *Middle East Tapestry*. Eugene, OR: Wipf & Stock, 2021.

———. *My Story*. Eugene, OR: Resource, 2023.

———. *Niebuhr in Egypt*. Eugene, OR: Pickwick, 2013.

Hobbes, Thomas. *The English Works of Thomas Hobbes of Malmesbury: Now First Collected and Edited by Sir William Molesworth, Bart*. Vol. 6. London: Bohn, 1840. https://oll.libertyfund.org/titles/hobbes-the-english-works-vol-vi-dialogue-behemoth-rhetoric.

Johnson, Samuel. *A Dictionary of the English Language: An Anthology*. London: Times, 1979. https://johnsonsdictionaryonline.com/.

Lane, Edward William. *An Account of the Manners and Customs of the Modern Egyptians*. 3rd ed. London: Ward, Lock & Co., n.d., ca. 1842. https://www.gutenberg.org/cache/epub/70796/pg70796-images.html.

Lawrence, T. E. *Seven Pillars of Wisdom: A Triumph*. Harmondsworth, UK: Penguin, 1963. https://archive.org/details/bwb_KR-055-777/mode/2up.

Lorimer, John Gordon. *Gazetteer of the Persian Gulf, Oman, and Central Arabia*. Westmead, UK: Gregg International; Shannon, UK: Irish University Press, 1970.

Malcolm, Noel. *Kosovo: A Short History*. New York: Harper Perennial, 1999.

Meinertzhagen, Richard. *Army Diary 1899–1926*. Edinburgh: Oliver and Boyd, 1960.

———. *Middle East Diary, 1917–1956*. London: Cresset, 1959.

———. *Nicoll's Birds of Egypt*. London: Rees, 1930.

Niebuhr, Carsten. *Reisebeschreibung nach Arabien und andern umliegenden Ländern*. Vol. 1. Copenhagen: Möller, 1774. https://digi.ub.uni-heidelberg.de/diglit/niebuhr1774abd1.

———. *Travels Through Arabia, and Other Countries in the East*. Vol. 1, translated by Robert Heron. Edinburgh: Mudie, 1792. https://archive.org/details/bim_eighteenth-century_travels-through-arabia-_niebuhr-carsten_1792_1/page/n5/mode/2up.

Rasmussen, Stig T., ed. *Den Arabiske Rejse 1761–1767: En dansk ekspedition set i videnskabshistorisk perspektiv*. Copenhagen: Munksgaard, 1990.

Richardson, Tony, dir. *Tom Jones*. UK: Woodfall Film Productions, 1963.

Robinson, Edward. *Biblical Researches in Palestine, Mount Sinai and Arabia Petraea: A Journal of Travels in the Year 1838*. Vol. 1. London: Murray, 1841. https://archive.org/details/in.ernet.dli.2015.32679/mode/2up.

———. *Biblical Researches in Palestine, Mount Sinai and Arabia Petraea: A Journal of Travels in the Year 1838*. Vol. 2. London: Murray, 1841. https://archive.org/details/in.ernet.dli.2015.32680/mode/2up.

Sears, Edmund H. "It Came Upon the Midnight Clear." Hymnary, 1849. https://hymnary.org/text/it_came_upon_the_midnight_clear.

Serle, W., et al. *Collins Field Guide: Birds of West Africa*. New York: Penguin, 1988.

Silber, Laura, and Allan Little. *The Death of Yugoslavia*. London: Penguin; BBC, 1996.

Storrs, Ronald. *Orientations*. London: Nicholson & Watson, 1937.

Wade, John Francis. "O Come, All Ye Faithful" [Adeste fideles]. Hymnary, 1841. https://hymnary.org/text/o_come_all_ye_faithful_joyful_and_triumph.

Wesley, Charles. "Hark! The Herald Angels Sing." Hymnary, 1739. https://hymnary.org/text/hark_the_herald_angels_sing_glory_to.

Woodcock, Martin. *Collins Handguide to the Birds of the Indian Sub-Continent*. London: Collins, 1990.

Young, Fay. *Souvenir of the Opening of the Edinburgh Balmoral Hotel*. Glasgow: Insider, 1991.

www.ingramcontent.com/pod-product-compliance
Lightning Source LLC
Chambersburg PA
CBHW072007060426
42446CB00042B/2017